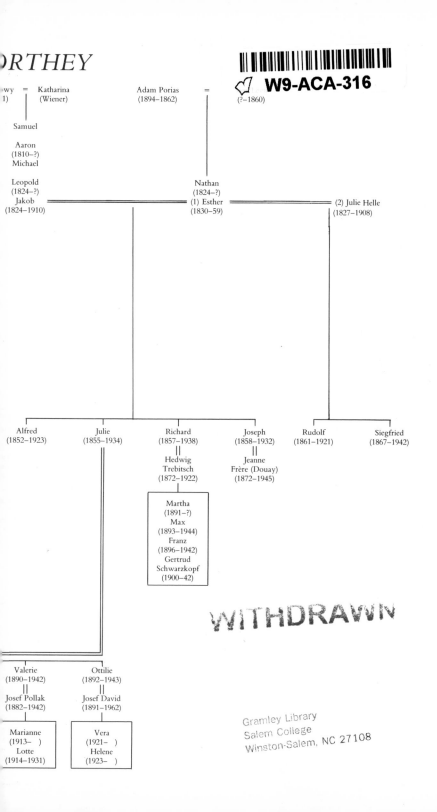

wy = Katharina
1) │ (Wiener)

Samuel

Aaron
(1810–?)
Michael

Leopold
(1824–?)
Jakob
(1824–1910)

Adam Porias
(1894–1862) = (?–1860)

Nathan
(1824–?)
(1) Esther
(1830–59) ══ (2) Julie Helle
(1827–1908)

Alfred
(1852–1923)

Julie
(1855–1934)

Richard
(1857–1938)
‖
Hedwig
Trebitsch
(1872–1922)

Martha
(1891–?)
Max
(1893–1944)
Franz
(1896–1942)
Gertrud
Schwarzkopf
(1900–42)

Joseph
(1858–1932)
‖
Jeanne
Frère (Douay)
(1872–1945)

Rudolf
(1861–1921)

Siegfried
(1867–1942)

Valerie
(1890–1942)
‖
Josef Pollak
(1882–1942)

Marianne
(1913–)
Lotte
(1914–1931)

Ottilie
(1892–1943)
‖
Josef David
(1891–1962)

Vera
(1921–)
Helene
(1923–)

KAFKA'S RELATIVES

Street café on the Josefplatz in Prague, *c*.1907

KAFKA'S RELATIVES
Their Lives and His Writing

ANTHONY NORTHEY

Yale University Press
New Haven and London
1991

To my parents

Set in Linotron Bembo by Excel Typesetting Company, Hong Kong and
printed and bound in Great Britain at The Bath Press, Avon,
Great Britain

Library of Congress Cataloging-in-Publication Data
Northey, Anthony, 1942–
[Kafkas Mischpoche. English]
Kafka's relatives; their lives and his writing/Anthony
Northey
Translation of: Kafkas Mischpoche.
Includes index
1. Kafka, Franz 1883-1924—Biography—Family.
2. Authors, Austrian—20th century—Biography.
I. Title
PT2621.A26Z811513   1990   833'.912—dc20   [B] 90-38268
ISBN   0-300-04585-9

Contents

Studio portraits of the Kafka family taken in 1910; top: Hermann and Julie, Franz's mother and father; middle: Franz and his sister Ottla; bottom: sisters Valerie (Valli) and Gabriele (Elli)

1
Kafka's Family Feeling

In the opening pages of his famous 'Letter to His Father', Franz Kafka lists a number of failings with which Hermann Kafka had reproached him, among them his lack of family feeling. What his father meant by 'family feeling' was not merely love and concern for one's immediate family but also a readiness to behave like a worthy representative of that family among one's legions of relatives. So 'family' included all relatives, who were held in varying degrees of esteem and against whom one measured one's own success. Franz Kafka was always ready to admit to himself as well as others that his father was justified in reproaching him for lack of family feeling. Compiling points for and against marriage in a diary entry for July 1913, he writes, 'the sorrows and joys of my relatives bore me to my soul' (D 225)[1]. Certainly he saw himself as much an outsider in the narrow circle of his family as he was in the wider one of his relations – and in the world in general – and he often described himself as such. Yet this characteristic, so often emphasized by Kafka himself and by his biographers, obscures a very different tendency: his interest in, even his love for, his relatives.

  This book will introduce some of Kafka's relations, some close to the family, others further removed. The Yiddish word *mishpocheh*, or clan, aptly describes this extended family, which includes those related by marriage as well as those by blood. Leo Rosten's semi-serious book *The Joys of Yiddish* even makes the claim that *mishpocheh* encompasses all Jews.[2] Kafka's acquaintance with Jizchak Löwy and a

1

troupe of Yiddish actors in 1911–12 gave him his first comprehensive introduction to the language and aroused his interest in it. Yiddish was probably not spoken in the Kafka household – because of its association with the *shtetl* it tended to be shunned by assimilated Jews who seldom used it in public – but words of *Jargon*, as it was called in Prague, were no doubt used by the Kafkas quite regularly. (This view is also held by Leopold Kreitner, who knew the family.)[3] Kafka records, for example, that his father called his friend Max Brod, for whom he had little time, a 'meshuggener Ritoch', a crazy fool, and he did this before the assembled family (*D* 98).

The word *mishpocheh* seems to have been routinely employed within the family. Julie Kafka uses it in her letter to Anna Bauer, the mother of her son's fiancée Felice, in August 1914, when she asks, 'Are none of your *mishpocheh* in the army?' (*LF* 435). It is in this neutral sense that the word is used here. For Kafka, words relating to family exemplified the inadequacy of German in the Jewish context: terms like *Mutter* or *Vater* could hardly convey the emotional nuances which for every Jew lay in those names (*D* 88). Yet he himself never used the word *mishpocheh* in his writings; typically, he preferred the cooler, more distanced German word, *Verwandtschaft*.

'Marrying, founding a family, accepting all the children that come, supporting them in this insecure world and even guiding them a little as well' – this was the 'utmost a human being can succeed in doing' (*W* 204). All his life it remained a challenge that Kafka could not rise to, despite the good patriarchal examples set by his father and preceding generations. The Kafka *mishpocheh* was large: Hermann had three brothers and two sisters; his mother Julie had three brothers and two half-brothers (see the genealogical chart on the endpapers). In the world administered by the Habsburg bureaucracy it was not easy to have such a substantial family, because the number of Jewish families in the Empire was subject to a strict quota (8,600 for Bohemia around 1815). Thus Hermann Kafka's elder brother and sister, Filip and Anna, were listed in the Jewish birth register as illegitimate until their father acquired a quota number and with

Kafka's grandparents: Joseph Kafka, the butcher from Wossek, and his wife Franziska

Below: view of Pisek

Bottom: 'Im Jüdischen' Street in the lower town of Wossek: the Kafkas' house is in the background on the left

it the right to have a family.[4] These restrictions were abandoned with the dawning of a more liberal era in 1848. The families of Hermann's brothers and sisters were almost all large, whereas in Kafka's mother's family only two of her four brothers married and only one of those two had children. Going back one generation one finds again a sizeable number of big families, which provided a network of uncles, aunts and cousins further removed.

The Kafka family came originally from the southern Bohemian town of Pisek and is recorded in documents there dating back to the seventeenth century.[5] Hermann and his five brothers and sisters, though, were born in the nearby village of Wossek, in the Strakonitz administrative district. Although Franz Kafka's grandfather Jakob was said to have been the last Jew in Wossek at the time of his death in 1889, the village had had a relatively large Jewish community as recently as 1852: twenty families comprising ninety-five individuals and maintaining one synagogue.[6] (Strakonitz itself had twenty-five Jewish families, Pisek only eleven.) The children of Jakob Kafka, a *shochet* or Jewish ritual butcher, and his wife Franziska Platowski grew up in poverty, but all of them became middle class by virtue of their intelligence and hard work. Kafka's mother's side of the family seems to have been better off financially. Certainly her father Jakob (1826–1910), who came from Humpoletz and opened a draper's shop in the town of Podiebrad east of Prague in 1860, could afford to hire a servant-girl.[7] In the 1870s he moved his family to Prague and went into business as a hop merchant.[8]

When Hermann Kafka measured his son's accomplishments against those of other members of the *mishpocheh,* he did so in terms of success in business. Thanks to the ability and diligence characteristic of the Kafkas, and also to a wise marriage, he had in the 1880s built up a retail (later wholesale) business in Prague dealing in fancy goods. Again and again he rebuked his seemingly spineless son, pointing to his own deprived youth as the ideal way to strengthen character. Even after he had established himself in business his struggle persisted, because he now had to maintain his success, and he did not hesitate to let his family know, through his complaints and reproaches, how much the effort cost him. From time to time he pressed Franz into service, whether to plead with one of the employees to return to the shop after being fired in a fit of anger (*D* 78) or to prevail upon another to agree to a minor insurance fraud (*D* 127). The 'ultimo', the day on which all bills fell due, was recalled by Franz as an ever recurring family crisis, familiar from his earliest childhood (*D* 146). So it is not surprising that the world of business, with its unremitting demand for results and its incessant deadlines, often provides the setting for Kafka's works. One has only to think of his many stories and story fragments in which the central figure is a harassed businessman. But although he usually paints an unflattering picture of the world of business Kafka had not always disliked the idea of a conventional career. As a young man he had hoped to become a success, like so many others in the *mishpocheh* whose lives – interesting chronicles in themselves – touched his and which he drew on for his fiction; indeed he occasionally hinted at these factual sources in the text itself.

Left: Alfred Loewy; above: Philippe Bunau-Varilla

Podiebrad market-place, c.1880

2

Into the Belle Époque:
The Loewys in Paris and Panama

When Franz Kafka completed his one year of articles with the lawyer Dr Richard Löwy (no relation), he seemed to have no prospects beyond unemployment. He considered making use of his period of joblessness to obtain his school-leaving certificate at the Commercial College (Handelsaka-demie) in Prague or to study at the Exportakademie in Vienna. To his friend Max Brod he wrote in August 1907, 'my uncle would have to find us a position in Spain, or else we would go to South America or the Azores, to Madeira' (L 25). In spite of the jocular tone Kafka strikes here, he genuinely longed to be 'looking out of the office windows at fields of sugar cane or Mohammedan cemeteries' (L 35), and his expectation of help from his uncle Alfred in Madrid was not completely misplaced, because Alfred was much ad-mired by his family and was often asked for advice.

Alfred and his younger brother Joseph had achieved honour and riches abroad. In his biography of Kafka Max Brod reports that Alfred worked his way up to become managing director of the Spanish railway system and that Joseph ran a company exporting exotic goods from the Congo and had outfitted caravans in those regions.[1] Both statements are false, or at least exaggerated, but they are very telling. Brod had obtained his information from the writer's mother,[2] whose inclination to inflate her brothers in this way reveals the admiration she felt for them. The truth

7

was somewhat less exotic but no less interesting. Both Alfred's and Joseph's careers offer classic examples of how Jews from modest provincial backgrounds were able to advance themselves at the time of the great capitalist, colonial expansion at the end of the last century. Their achievements, attained after great sacrifice, were extraordinary. It is doubtful whether Franz Kafka would actually have had the fortitude or the desire to follow their paths.

Alfred Loewy was born in 1852 in the little Bohemian town of Podiebrad, the son of Jakob and Esther Löwy; his brother Joseph, the couple's last child, was born in the same town in 1858.[3] Both chose to enter the world of business and (according to their own statements) attended the Commercial College in Prague. In 1873 Alfred moved to Vienna to work as a bookkeeper in the firm of Lipstadt & Co. and three years later went on to Paris, where he was offered a position as *fondé de pouvoirs* (chief clerk or *Prokurist*) in the banking house of Maurice Bunau-Varilla, financier and owner of the Paris newspaper *Le Matin*. Joseph completed his year of practical training in the little Bohemian town of Hořovice and, as the note registering his passport application in the Political Business Protocol of the District Office of Podiebrad suggests, he left Prague in 1882, probably to join the Bunau-Varilla business in the French capital on the recommendation of his brother. On 15 February, 1881, however, the *Bulletin du Canal Interocéanique* listed the arrival of a 'M. Lévy, chef du service de la comptabilité à l'agence supérieure à Panama' on the packet ship *Ville-de-Bordeaux*.[4] Since this French spelling of Loewy's name appears in the passport-entry in his native Bohemia – an unusual spelling for Austrian bureaucracy – it can be assumed that the newspaper was indeed referring to Joseph Loewy and that the entry in the protocol of Podiebrad occurred incorrectly under the year 1882 instead of 1881.

Here a word of explanation is called for about the Bunau-Varillas, especially about Philippe (Maurice's younger brother), who did most to further the careers of the Loewy brothers. Today the name of Philippe Bunau-Varilla is hardly remembered, yet it was through his efforts that the United States secured control over the Panama Canal in the

Hay–Varilla Treaty, domination which was voluntarily relinquished only in recent times.[5]

Born in 1860, Philippe Bunau-Varilla attended the well-known École Polytechnique in Paris and became – because, one historian claims, he was able to survive the murderous climate – chief engineer of the French Panama Canal Company, the Compagnie Universelle du Canal Interocéanique de Panama. It was during this period that his two Bohemian protégés proved most useful to him. To gain a lucrative source of income, Philippe Bunau-Varilla invested in Artigue, Sonderegger & Co., a company founded by former Canal Company employees which drew up excavation contracts with the French company. 'Travaux du Canal de Panama', the letterhead of the private company proclaimed proudly, listing the locations of its offices as Paris, Colón, Culebra and Panama.[6] According to a letter of recommendation written many years later, Joseph Loewy was active in a commercial venture in Panama and, since his name appears nowhere in the lists of the Compagnie Universelle du Canal Interocéanique, it seems plausible that he worked for Artigue, Sonderegger & Co., standing in for Bunau-Varilla, who, despite the more liberal financial climate of the times, probably did not want to draw attention to the obvious conflict of interest between his position as a high official of the French Canal Company and his private money-making venture.[7] (A statement by Theodore Roosevelt in later years also places brother Alfred at the scene of the Panama Canal undertaking, but more about Roosevelt's words later.)

The outcome of the French canal-building effort was a débâcle unparalleled in France's history. Attracted and even blinded by the name of the famous builder of the Suez Canal, Ferdinand de Lesseps, who now headed the Panama Company, thousands of Frenchmen, especially the petite bourgeoisie, had invested millions of francs in the venture by buying shares and bonds made even more attractive by a government-sanctioned lottery. But in 1889, after nine years of mismanagement, lack of funds forced a halt to the construction, and the decision to investigate what had happened to the investment money led to the scandal of

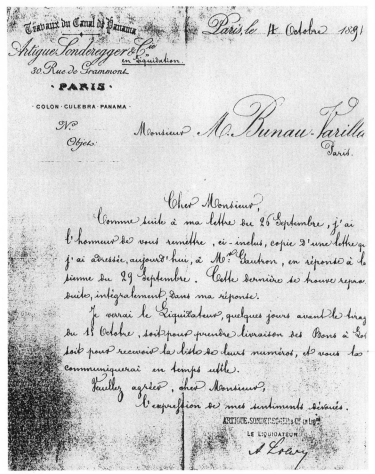

A letter from Alfred Loewy to Philippe Bunau-Varilla

'l'affaire Panama'. It ended with a parliamentary investigation, with prison sentences for some of the participants, including de Lesseps, and with penalties imposed on companies which had allegedly enriched themselves at the expense of others. But many questions remained unanswered, and the name *panamiste* was coined as a term of abuse meaning swindler.[8]

With no earth or rock to move, the firm of Artigue, Sonderegger & Co. was forced into liquidation. The man

The construction of the Panama Canal, *c.*1898

entrusted with this process was none other than Alfred Loewy, who dealt with J.P. Gautron, the chief representative of the government, in charge of deciding which firms had to be fined and how much.[9] The loss, although painful for the Bunau-Varillas, was by no means fatal. In succeeding years they proved that they had enough financial backing to weather the storm and invest elsewhere, in Spain and in the Congo. Partly because of a sincere belief that the canal was viable and a boon for mankind, partly because of his dogged determination to turn a temporary defeat into a victory, Philippe Bunau-Varilla pursued the idea of the Panama Canal into the first decade of the twentieth century. With true French *élan* and by means of a clever propaganda campaign and outright bribes, he eventually brought the United States Congress over to his way of thinking. Knowing all the twists and turns of the path on the way to his goal enabled him to profit from the fluctuations of Panama Company stock.

Yet the Panama scandal had a darker side, which affected the Bunau-Varillas and consequently the Loewys. Since Jews had been involved in the selling of shares for the French Canal Company – in particular the financier Baron de Reinach, the dynamite manufacturer Arton and an American swindler named Cornelius Herz – the fury of the French public, inflamed by anti-Semitic papers like *La Libre Parole*, was vented on Jews in general. 'L'affaire Panama' can be seen as the beginning of the anti-Semitic wave which soon swept over France during the Belle Époque and spilled over into a much more bitter *affaire*, the case of the army Captain Alfred Dreyfus.

Philippe Bunau-Varilla himself saw a clear connection between the two *affaires*. In August 1906 he wrote an open letter to the editor-in-chief of the New York *Evening Post* counter-attacking the editor of the scandal-sheet *La Libre Parole*:

You may see now with what men you have joined in your attacks against me, and you may also begin to understand that the 'Dreyfus affaire' and the 'Panama affaire' are but two phases of the same war on the republican form of government in France. You will find in both the same men, the same falsehoods, the same forgeries. These criminals wrecked greatest private-enterprize of France: Panama and made a convict of an innocent: Dreyfus.[10]

Only a short time before, on 26 June, Alfred Loewy had made the same connection in a letter to his protector, attacking another extreme nationalist and anti-Dreyfusard, Ernest Judet, editor of *Le Petit Journal*: 'His [Judet's] nationalistic policy, whose fruits have been the injustices of the Dreyfus trial and the ruin of the French oceanic canal undertaking, would put him to shame if only he had a modicum of sense.'[11] Perhaps these words merely echoed a view often expressed by Bunau-Varilla. In any case, it would have been natural for him as a Jew, assimilated or not, to feel threatened by the hostile world around him.

Moreover, it should be mentioned that the two Varilla brothers were not ineffectual bystanders in the Dreyfus scandal. They intervened actively on the Captain's side. Dreyfus had been Philippe's classmate at the École Polytechnique and had written to him about an engineering problem which had cropped up in the construction of the Congo Railway, of which Philippe had some knowledge. It was Philippe who years later hit upon the idea of comparing the handwriting on the infamous *bordereau*, the central piece of evidence against the accused Captain, with that of the letter. The comparison, which exonerated Dreyfus and led eventually to his rehabilitation, was made public in Maurice Bunau-Varilla's *Le Matin*.[12] Both brothers had openly committed themselves in the bitterest of wars, which had pitted Dreyfusards against anti-Dreyfusards.

It was not only at the high point of the Dreyfus trial that they exposed themselves to the attacks of Jew-baiters. Twelve years before they had come under fire from the same *Libre Parole* in its campaign against what it saw as inordinate Jewish influence in the development of the Belgian Congo. An article from the year 1894 entitled 'Le Congo belge aux juifs' reads in part, 'One sees Israelite capital flowing into the Congo venture; the Lambert-Rothschilds, the Philippson-Horwitzes, the de Bauers, the Bleichroeders of Berlin, the Oppenheims of Cologne, the Bunau-Varillas of Paris and Panama are gaining the upper hand and giving it that great Jewish–Freemasonic nationality.'[13]

Because of the high profile adopted by their patrons in the anti-Semitic tumult, the Loewys could not help but feel exposed, at the mercy of Jew-haters and doubly dependent on the protection of the Varillas. Presumably to shield their employees, but perhaps also to avoid embarrassing questions about their business in Panama, the Varilla brothers decided to find positions abroad for Alfred and Joseph.

Matadi station at the inauguration of the Matadi–Stanley Pool section of Congo Railway, June 1898. It is possible Loewy is the man sitting second from the right.

3

From Matadi to Montreux: The Life of Joseph Loewy

On 31 January 1891, at the port of Ostend, Joseph Loewy boarded the steamer *Belgian Prince* bound for the Congo to take up his post as *agent commercial* for the Société Anonyme Belge pour le Commerce du Haut Congo.[1] At the Berlin Conference of 1885 the Congo had been assigned to Léopold II, King of the Belgians and, although it was officially designated 'l'État indépendant du Congo', it was to all intents and purposes his personal fief. Newly founded Belgian trading companies (which eventually squeezed out most of the foreign companies) began to explore and then exploit the vast regions. They were searching in particular for minerals, ivory, rubber and plant oils along the various tributaries of the Congo river. It was a perfect opportunity for earning money and making careers.

This meant not only exciting adventure but also hardship, distress and danger. All the necessities of European life had to be shipped in at great cost. At first the colonizers did not have even the most basic materials and, not knowing what was suitable for their new environment, they let themselves in for some costly experiments.

When the Belgians, and traders from other nations, began their exploitation of the Congo region, they were intruding on the turf of local traders, Arabs and tribal chieftains, who for years had conducted a brisk commerce in exotic wares, including slaves. Confrontation between the large- and small-scale capitalists ensued when the latter, seeing the erosion of their trade, incited various tribes to rise up against the European intruders. In the early 1890s, for example, only a short time after Joseph Loewy had arrived in Africa, the uprising at Riba-Riba took place in which trading posts were overrun and their white occupants massacred. According to contemporary reports of these attacks, there were even isolated cases of cannibalism.[2] It was around this time that Joseph Conrad worked for the Belgians on a small steamer on the Congo river before being sent home following an attack of fever. Many of the impressions he gathered there went into his sombre and terrifying novella *Heart of Darkness*.

Joseph Loewy owed his job with the Société Anonyme primarily to the friendship between Philippe Bunau-Varilla and Captain (later General) Albert Thys, King Léopold's right-hand man in his African colony.[3] The company had been set up on 10 December 1888 as a subsidiary of the Compagnie du Congo pour le Commerce et l'Industrie, itself founded only a short time before, and its main function was to supply the workers on the planned Congo Railway with food. It was said that Thys guaranteed posts for both of

The Congo railway under construction

16

the Varilla brothers on the administrative council of the
Congo Railway because he feared that Maurice would
otherwise mount a massive propaganda offensive in his
scandal-sheet *Le Matin*. The paper had already published an
article claiming among other things that 'After Stanley and
the Belgians, civilization in Africa has been thrown back half
a century.' In this instance Thys was able to limit the
damage; in an altercation some years later he could not
prevent Maurice from describing King Léopold as 'a
desiccated soul, infinitely egotistical, profit-hungry, a plun-
derer of ivory and rubber'.[4] In the early 1890s, at a time
when he was desperately attempting to drum up capital to
develop the Congo, Thys clearly feared that men of power
and influence like the Varillas could sabotage his efforts in
France with this sort of advertisement.

It had become evident after the first exploratory expedi-
tion that a railway would be the best way to by-pass the
long stretch of the Congo river between Matadi and Stanley
Pool which was rendered unnavigable by rapids and
waterfalls. Raw materials could then be transported the 400
kilometres from the interior by rail instead of by the
inefficient and even fatal caravans used hitherto, and those

Bridge across a ravine on the Congo railway

17

articles needed for the expanding railway system and the colonizing effort generally could be shipped in. As in the construction of the Panama Canal there were huge and diverse natural obstacles to be overcome: in some parts steep hillsides with forbidding gradients and ravines, or steamy, swampy terrain overrun with vegetation which took over building sites almost as soon as it had been cleared away. To many politicians, private investors and newspaper people in Belgium and in Europe generally, the hurdles faced by contemporary technology seemed insurmountable, and the projected railway in the Congo was dubbed 'le tramway jou-jou', the toy train.

In September 1892 Joseph Loewy transferred from the Société Anonyme to the Compagnie du Chemin de Fer du Congo, where by March 1893 he had risen to the position of *chef comptable*, chief bookkeeper, in Matadi, the settlement at the foot of the unnavigable part of the river and at the start of the projected railway line. His rapid rise is testimony at once to his ability and to the severe shortage of personnel. The company was often forced to employ men of mediocre abilities,[5] so it was easy for the Bohemian bookkeeper to outshine the competition. Again, the Varilla–Thys connection may have played a part in Loewy's advancement. He was not the only Panama veteran whom Varilla managed to place in the Congo venture. The French engineers Espanet and Eymar and the Swiss Paggi and Burgi all held important posts with the railway; Espanet even became one of the two directors of the company in Africa, Thys' representative. They were nicknamed 'les panamistes', probably an ironic reference to the epithet doing the rounds in France in the wake of the Panama scandal.

'It was not a very cheerful life that I led at that time, working on the building of the railway in the interior of the Congo' (*W* 63): in this fashion Kafka begins a story in one of his octavo notebooks, a fragment obviously modelled on the career of his uncle. 'Mittleren Kongo' or 'middle Congo', not a term often used, corresponds to the geographical location of Matadi, and 'railway construction' to Loewy's job. But whether Loewy actually found life less than cheerful we cannot say. Certainly there was hardly anything for the whites or blacks employed in the venture to be cheerful about. The uprisings already mentioned caused no more than occasional periods of terror, but insufficient provisioning and the prevalence of illness ensured a degree of everyday misery. And the choice of illnesses was wide: dysentery, smallpox, swamp fever, beriberi, yellow fever, rheumatism, bilious fever, blood poisoning, to name only a few. Many Europeans suffered from a chronic slight fever. One is reminded of the narrator of Kafka's 'Memoirs of the Kalda Railway', who, having overcome a severe illness, cannot shake off a debilitating fever (*D* 312 – 13). Many of the new arrivals, healthy young Europeans, fell ill and died shortly after landing; in Loewy's bookkeeping department of some twenty to twenty-seven people, at least eight men in their twenties and thirties succumbed to disease, some very soon after arrival. Conditions were especially unbearable during the years 1891 to 1893 when the progress of construction from Matadi over the Palaballa mountain and across the M'pozo river was agonizingly slow. The names of the various construction camps, such as Camp of Death or Camp of Fever, reflect the despair the workers felt. Many of the blacks, some of whom had been recruited in highly dubious circumstances and shipped in almost as slaves, threw themselves into the river after the departing steamers in the hope of being fished out and taken back home. In December 1891 the black workers on the Congo Railway even mutinied and marched on Matadi intent on forcing their repatriation.[6]

The whites, of course, segregated themselves completely from the blacks, no doubt for the most part believing them, according to the prevailing attitudes, to be little better than animals. The Congo historian René J. Cornet tells of recruiters for black labour in other African countries who, unable to pronounce the African names of the men they were employing, took to baptizing them with new ones such as 'Bottel-beer' (*sic*), 'Black Pudding' or 'Baboon'. These names stuck and were even given official sanction in the employees' files after they entered the Congo.[7] There is no evidence that Joseph Loewy himself was a racist who subscribed to this demeaning practice, but it is quite possible

Life in Matadi in Loewy's day. Above: transporting the *maisons des agents* (see page 22) and right) provisions by rail. Above right: the town of Matadi showing the Company hou offices. Below: members of the *service comptabilité* during the 1890s

that he reported to his family about how blacks were treated in the Congo. A highly sensitive young Kafka could well have gathered impressions which years later found expression in his story 'A Report to an Academy'. Colonizers in the Congo were bent on educating those whom they considered little more than apes. Kafka, by contrast, chooses an intelligent, sensitive ape, Rotpeter, as the protagonist of his story, who after various degrading rituals is welcomed into 'civilized' human society and is forced thereby to give up a much more precious freedom.

Matadi, the 'city of stones', so called because it had been built on the piles of rock spewed forth by the rapids of the Congo river, was described by one European visitor, Edmond Picard, in 1896 as a desolate waste, with barracks that appeared like scabs among the mounds of rubble. 'Business! Business! Business!' and 'Profit, profit, nothing but profit' were according to Picard the two common denominators of the settlement, the motives which clearly determined everything in the colony. 'Yes, everything here has been arranged to promote this damnable profit, so much so that one wonders how worthwhile one's life can be in such a place, devoid as it is of all that can make it pleasant and desirable.'[8] He found the African bush, through which the railway was being built, no more enticing. A number of Kafka's heroes flee to similar regions.

The living quarters in Matadi, even for the senior personnel, were Spartan, not to say primitive. According to one account, rats (which make a prominent appearance in Kafka's 'Kalda Railway') infested the barracks of the main camp.[9] When the narrator of the Congo fragment in the octavo notebook speaks of his small wooden shack with its verandah covered by a fine-meshed mosquito net acquired from the chief of a native tribe, he comes very close to the truth. A photograph from the 1890s shows the small huts of the company traders, the *maisonettes des agents*, being transported on flatcars a little further down the newly laid railway line. One is reminded of the collapsible *maisons danoises*, which – according to a report in *Le Mouvement Géographique*, a colonial journal of the time – were modified in a unique way: 'When they intend to stay in the same spot for a certain amount of time and especially at the height of the hot season, the agents as a rule have the natives construct a third roof of grass which covers the whole house and which, projecting several metres from the front of the building, forms a sort of verandah under which one can take one's meals in the shade while remaining in the open air.'[10]

Joseph Loewy endured the hardships of the Congo for nearly twelve years. During this time he held some very important posts; from October 1893 until the end of November 1895 he was chief of the administrative offices in Africa; from May 1896 until the end of July, chief of the accounting departments; from November 1897 until April 1900 and from September of that year until March 1902, chief of the commercial sections of the railway. His stay there was, of course, broken up by the usual periods of leave. After eighteen months, at the most two years, every European was sent back home to recuperate for six months or more. Loewy first returned in 1893 (from March to September), thereafter in the years 1895–6, 1897 and 1900.[11] It is evident that his constitution – perhaps strengthened by his time in Panama – was a hardy one. No doubt Kafka, much as he may have wished to work in exotic places, realized very soon that such adventures would have been too much for his fragile health.

Life in the Congo became somewhat more bearable for everyone after the mid-1890s. In July 1896, at the opening of the first 200 kilometres of track at Tumba station, halfway between Matadi and Stanley Pool, Albert Thys could even provide colonial dignitaries and railway executives – among them Loewy – with a selection of the best European and exotic African dishes accompanied by fine French wines.[12] The next 200 kilometres were completed much more quickly, in slightly under two years. In May 1898 the first locomotive travelled from Matadi to Stanley Pool; following the grand opening in July of the same year, all the members of the *personnel supérieur* received decorations from Léopold. As head of an important department Loewy was granted the gold medal of the Ordre du Lion Royal.[13]

After the first stretch of rail had been laid, the various colonial companies set about exploiting the region. The

Inauguration of the Congo Railway by Louis van Engelen (detail); this was in July 1898 at Stanley Pool in the presence of Léopold. Joseph Loewy is probably the figure on the far left.

construction of other railways was started. The volume of exports and imports, which had already begun to rise rapidly before the first line had been completed, grew by leaps and bounds. So did the price of stock in the Compagnie du Chemin de Fer du Congo, shares rising from a low of 320 Belgian francs in 1894 to 1,500 francs in 1898 and 2,820 in 1900.[14] Loewy, well placed to judge the financial benefits brought by the railway, profited from dealing in its shares. After the 1898 inauguration he stayed on almost four years longer as head of the Service Commercial. In April 1902 he returned on the steamship *Albertville,* disembarking at Tenerife.[15] Yet, in all these years in important positions, Loewy attracted little attention. His name does not figure prominently in the many contemporary or modern descriptions of the construction of the Congo Railway; it hardly surfaces in official documents. That he is not mentioned in bulletins of Congo veterans' associations suggests that he kept to himself, that he did not feel he fitted in with the Belgian colonizers, and probably that he had few friends among the other officials in Africa.

The Belgian colonial export firms showed an ever increasing independence, seeming to forget the debt they owed to the royal aegis. Even so, the Belgian public held the King responsible for abuses of human rights, forcing him to divest himself of the colony by turning it over to his country's government. Thus the days were numbered when men like Thys and the Bunau-Varillas could exercise unrestrained influence over events through their hand-picked subordinates. For Joseph Loewy an uncertain future loomed, and this probably made it easier for him to accept a new position.

The next stop for Kafka's uncle was China, which towards the end of the nineteenth century had become the new arena of European capital investment. Highly developed though the country was culturally, technologically it was still in the Middle Ages. The atrophied imperial governmental structure had only nominal control over the vast country: its influence in the peripheral areas and in the vassal states had crumbled. As Kafka showed in his Chinese stories, the voice of the Emperor (actually of the Dowager Empress) was very remote and had less force in the provinces than that of the provincial governors. Foreign powers had defeated China in several wars and had carved it

The inauguration celebrations at the *maison des compatables* at Matadi were more modest.

up into spheres of influence, where they had strong control over commerce and their own independent judicial systems without regard for the sovereignty of the Chinese.[16]

The foreign powers, headed by France, Great Britain, Germany, Russia and the United States, vied with each other to gain concessions to construct railway lines, partly to open new markets, partly to expand their areas of influence and military control, and – as they had in the Congo – to exploit the natural resources. These railways would by and large replace the old transport routes: roads in the north, rivers in the south, some hardly passable at the best of times and especially vulnerable in bad weather. The Chinese authorities, who were by no means convinced of the benefits of modern western technology, were persuaded, some say coerced, into concluding lucrative contracts for various stretches of railroad. As in Kafka's story 'The Great Wall of China', the construction went on in sections all over the country.

The Belgians also took part in the hunt for concessions and were rewarded with the 1,200 kilometre Peking-to-Hankow line. The Chinese gave them this construction project in order to avoid having to award it to the French, to whom they had just surrendered Annam (later Vietnam). Léopold II, who hoped to increase Belgium's role in bringing technology to China, sent Albert Thys to start the building of the Chengtai branch line. Thys relied on a pool of proven Congo veterans to help him in this undertaking, engineers like Georges Espanet, for example. Joseph Loewy came to China as an employee of the Banque Russo-Chinoise[17] – a misleading name, for the bank had little to do with Russia and less with China. Its capital was supplied mainly by Belgian and French financiers.[18]

Exactly how Loewy obtained his position with the bank and where he was stationed in China is not known. A passenger list in the *North China Herald* shows that he travelled from Shanghai to Hankow in mid-October 1903 on the steamer *Mei Lee* and left that city for Chefoo at the end of November on the steamer *Shenking*. In a letter dated 8 February 1904 to Georges Espanet, Director of the Imperial Shansi Railway in Peking, Philippe Bunau-Varilla

Left: officer on the *Mei Lee*. Below: two views of the Peking-Hankow line *c.*1900

asks that his best wishes be passed on to Loewy, an indication that the latter was still in China at that time.[19]

A consular report of the year 1900 about personnel recruitment suggests that the administrative structure of the Banque Russo-Chinoise was as loose as that of the huge country in which it operated. The bank employee, it states, 'is not part of an administrative hierarchy, but is in the service of a bank which has numerous branches but lacks the management personnel to direct them, and has difficulty keeping in that far-off country the few agents with whom it is satisfied'.[20] The report recommended that new young recruits should have a private income, so that they could preserve a modicum of independence abroad.

Joseph Loewy returned to Europe before 1906. In France he married Jeanne Douay, who had been born in Ghent in 1872 but had been living in Versailles since before the turn of the century.[21] Loewy's wealth was probably considerable at that time and although he did not move in the same circles as the Bunau-Varillas and Thys, they no doubt helped him with well-timed financial advice. Again it is likely to have been Thys who in the autumn of 1907 had Loewy appointed Administrative Director of the Crédit Municipal Canadien in Montreal. This private company invested capital in municipal projects in Montreal and elsewhere in the province of Quebec: water supply, sewage disposal and electrification. It had been founded in 1903 by prominent French–Canadian businessmen, who acted as a front for Belgian money from what had become known as 'le groupe Thys'. It is no surprise to find another of Joseph's colleagues at the Banque Russo-Chinoise, the director C.R. Wehrung, appearing on the board of directors of the Canadian company.[22]

Crédit Municipal's attempt to gain a foothold in Quebec failed. In fact, when Loewy came to Canada in October 1908 his actual task was to sell the company's assets. Although for most of his stay he lived in Montreal, in the suburb of Lachine, where Crédit Municipal had property, he travelled elsewhere in Quebec, notably to the town of Rimouski about 100 kilometres downstream from the city of Quebec. There he negotiated the sale of a generating station which provided the inhabitants of the town with an inadequate supply of electricity at enormous expense, much to their dissatisfaction. (Correspondence with town officials shows that Loewy visited Rimouski in the autumn of 1908.)[23] Thus three years before Kafka began his novel *Amerika,* he had an uncle living in North America.

In 1910 a dispute arose between Loewy and his employees when he deducted his commission before actually selling a property in St Romuald, Quebec. Since Crédit Municipal had been about to take a loss on the property, he had probably wanted to make sure of being paid. The matter came before a Quebec arbitration board, which decided in the company's favour. After this unpleasant affair, Loewy seems to have retired from active business. He took up residence in a rented villa in Versailles and spent the summer months in the fashionable seaside resort of St Malo/St Servan. Although thanks to his domicile he has been characterized as Kafka's 'French' uncle, Joseph Loewy never applied to become a naturalized French citizen. Consequently, he and his wife, who had acquired Austrian citizenship by her marriage to him, were treated as enemy aliens at the outbreak of the First World War and detained in St Servan until 1918. Around 1928 the couple moved to Switzerland. Loewy died in Montreux in November 1932 and was buried in the Catholic cemetery of Les Troches.[24]

Personal contact between Franz Kafka and his uncle Joseph, unlike that with Alfred Loewy, cannot be documented. Joseph probably visited Prague in the 1890s and early 1900s before his marriage, thus pre-dating Kafka's diary and the main body of his letters, which are the only places where such family matters are recorded. As mentioned before, Europeans working in the Congo spent several months at home recuperating, and Loewy undoubtedly returned to Prague to visit his parents. Kafka might have seen him in Paris on one of his two trips to that city in 1910 and 1911. That Kafka's sister Ottla and her husband Josef David paid Uncle Joseph and his wife a visit in June 1921 demonstrates that the bonds between the Kafkas in Prague and Loewy were strong enough to survive the four years of war, during which communication between enemy countries was very difficult. Julie Kafka too stayed with her brother in 1923 when she travelled to Versailles to collect her portion of Alfred Loewy's inheritance, which Joseph had looked after. Even if Kafka had little or no personal contact with Joseph Loewy, he may have heard a great deal about his uncle's adventurous life through his uncle Alfred in Madrid, who certainly saw his brother frequently in Paris – in June 1914, for example, shortly before he continued on his way to Prague.

4

On the Pirates' Galley: The Career of Alfred Loewy

In 1890 Alfred Loewy became a French citizen.[1] In his application for citizenship he gave 'sympathie pour la France' as a reason for his wish to change nationality, and in an accompanying, slightly more detailed letter referred to 'mon amour sincère de la France et mon attachement à ses institutions'. Perhaps the immigration authorities were no less convinced by his annual salary of 15,000 francs as *fondé de pouvoirs* in the bank of Maurice Bunau-Varilla and by the balance in his bank account of 50,000 francs.

Around 1895 Loewy became Director of the railway company Compañia de los Ferrocariles de Madrid a Cáceres y Portugal y del Oeste de España. At the same time he acted as representative for the Medina del Campo a Salamanca line (and before that also for the Compañia de Ferrocariles de Tarragona a Barcelona i Franca). The post of director at the Madrid a Cáceres came to him thanks to his acquaintance with Philippe Bunau-Varilla. This Spanish railway had been created in 1894 by the fusion of two smaller lines which had run into financial difficulties and been purchased by a consortium headed by the Varilla brothers. There were some tricky problems to be solved in the construction of the Madrid a Cáceres line, for which Philippe Bunau-Varilla assembled an engineering team consisting of Panama veterans like Édouard Paggi and Georges Espanet, whom he later recommended to the Congo Railway.[2]

As Director, Alfred Loewy took charge of the day-to-day running of the company. But the impressive title did not mean that he had power, nor could it hide the railway's almost continual financial problems. Without the backing of solid profits from year to year, Loewy had to depend on the good will of his protector to sustain him in his job. How dependent and inconsequential he was became only too evident at the end of January 1902 when he learned unexpectedly from a source outside the company that – as he delicately put it in a letter to Varilla of 20 March – 'we are presently negotiating the sale of our railway line'.[3] In the all-inclusive 'we' there lay the reproach that he had not been informed. 'I cannot hide from you', his letter continues,

> the fact that if you come down in favour of the course suggested by M. de Guada, I will be gravely affected by it, but I would like to hope that, should the sale go through, you will be able to put my physical and intellectual abilities to good use in a new enterprise. If not, I obviously have no other option but to remain with M. Arnus & Co., with the certain knowledge that this would not be for long, since these gentlemen have for the position of director or general secretary far too many capable personal friends, at least as capable as I.

Five months after this letter was written, the young Franz Kafka asked his uncle, who was in Prague on a visit, to 'guide me to some place where at last I could start afresh' (*L* 4). He obviously wanted his admired uncle to find him a job abroad and so liberate him from his native Prague, 'this old crone with claws'. He received a non-committal answer which promised no tangible help. Alfred Loewy's own precarious position meant that he was hardly in a position to offer his nephew advice, let alone a job, having just had to beg for his own.

Bunau-Varilla saw to it that Loewy kept his directorship, even after the Madrid a Cáceres had changed hands, and in 1907 Uncle Alfred was finally able to help Franz. Although he could not use his influence to obtain a job for him in a foreign country as his nephew had wished, he did use his connections to get him his first employment with the Assicurazioni Generali insurance company in Prague. In Madrid Loewy had also been active in the insurance

Free pass for the President of the Compañia de los Ferrocariles
Madrid a Cácares y Portugal, Philippe Bunau-Varilla, also signed
by Alfred Loewy

business; he was *administrador delegado* of the Mutualidad
Española. An acquaintance, José Arnaldo Weissberger,
representative of the Generali in Madrid, had his father
Arnold, the American Honorary Consul in Prague, put in a
good word for Kafka at the Prague branch.[4]

From their position of power the Bunau-Varilla brothers
could demand unflinching loyalty from their subordinates.
Philippe was reported to have been an arrogant publicity-
seeker; Maurice, banker and newspaper-owner, was wont
to remark, 'My office chair is worth three royal thrones.'[5]
We have already mentioned that Albert Thys brought the
two Varillas on to the administrative council of the
Compagnie du Chemin de Fer du Congo in order to avoid a
nasty publicity campaign against the Congo venture. In his
book *Du Bluff au Chantage* (*From Bluff to Blackmail*), written
in 1908, François Ignace Mouthon, a former employee of *Le
Matin*, described a number of 'les grandes campagnes du
Matin', incidents in which the newspaper had fanned the
flames of scandal, real or imagined, with sensationalism.
Mouthon brought up the murky financial dealings connected with Panama and the Congo and told how his editor,
Varilla, had manipulated the employees into taking part in

his defamatory campaigns. 'All those whom I knew on this galley', he wrote about his fellow workers at *Le Matin*, 'were very decent people, who rowed, some with more, some with less enthusiasm for the profit of a pirate.'[6] (Years later, opportunism and a fear and hatred of Bolshevism drove Maurice to put his newspaper at the disposal of the Nazi occupation forces, which at the liberation of France in 1944 almost earned him a place in front of a firing squad.)

Unlike Mouthon, Loewy did not rebel, but remained grateful and subservient. In his struggle to convince the United States, especially the American Congress, of the importance of constructing an inter-oceanic canal and placing it where he wanted it, across the Isthmus of Panama, Philippe Bunau-Varilla was able to use his trusty servant to run errands in Madrid libraries looking up documents important to his argument. Loewy was always ready to send his patron a flattering telegram or letter congratulating him on his victories or commiserating with him on his defeats and inveighing against his foes. His comment on the newspaper editor Judet has already been quoted, words that seem sober in comparison with the ardour of some of his other eulogies. Here are some examples, which illuminate not only Loewy's relationship with Varilla but also his personality:

when I found reunited in your eloquent appeal the names of Panama and of the great Frenchman [de Lesseps] there appeared before me the vision of Golgotha and Christ, whom an ignorant and fanatical people had made to suffer a thousand deaths and to empty the cup of ignominy to the dregs. . . . Golgotha! – Panama! The miracle which was wrought in one will be wrought in the other. The mighty plan of Ferdinand de Lesseps will have its day of resurrection and Panama will become synonymous with all that is great, all that is noble, all that is sublime on this earth. And you will have had a large, a very large, part in it. Forgive me for raising my modest voice, but I cannot silence my feelings.

Varilla must have been moved by this religious metaphor, for in 1913 he gave to his lengthy justification of the French canal venture and his own efforts the title 'Panama: la création, la destruction et la résurrection'. In another letter, Loewy turns to the Old Testament for a model with which to compare his benefactor. He writes, 'Nonetheless, I have

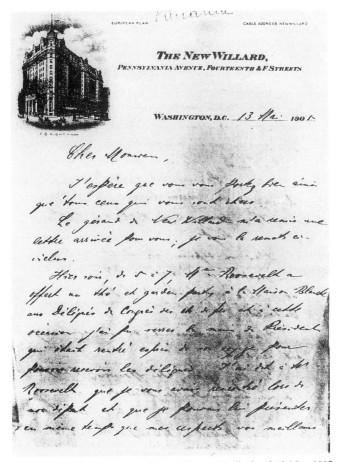

Letter from Alfred Loewy to Philippe Bunau-Varilla dated 13 May 1905 telling him he had spoken to President Roosevelt at a garden party at the White House the day before

confidence in your star and in imminent justice. A new Moses, you will show us the Promised Land and the path which leads there, but, more fortunate than he, it will be given to you to enter it. And I can only hope to be among your following.'[7] It is significant in assessing Philippe Bunau-Varilla's personality that he found these flattering letters important enough to keep for many years, finally including them in the papers which he gave to the Library of

Congress at the end of his life. Mouthon too attests to Varilla's penchant for collecting testimonials.

A similarly orotund style with a dash of benevolent paternal condescension can be found in a letter that Uncle Alfred wrote to his newly engaged nephew and his fiancée Felice Bauer on 14 May 1914. 'Your affectionate, joint, undated letter (happy people don't count the days) came as a delightful surprise; it sounds like a lovers' duet, and will be preserved not as a letter but as a piece of music' (*LF* 413). This overpolished mode of expression conformed with Loewy's appearance, depicted with loving irony in Kafka's diary entry for 4 September 1912: 'My uncle from Spain. The cut of his coat. The effect of his nearness. The details of his personality. His floating through the ante-room into the toilet, in the course of which he makes no reply to what is said to him. Becomes milder from day to day, if one judges not in terms of a gradual change but the moments which stand out.' (*D* 208) Kafka had, of course, recognized the great importance of exterior form in his uncle's life. At the beginning of his visit he seemed more like an official. A day later the young man asked his uncle how he managed to square with his outward success his admitted dissatisfaction with life – a burning question for Kafka, whose much deeper dissatisfaction with his life thwarted all ambition. 'In individual things I am dissatisfied,' Alfred replied,

this doesn't extend to the whole. I often dine in a little French pension that is very exclusive and expensive. For example, a room for a couple, with meals, costs fifty francs a day. So I sit there between the secretary of the French legation, for example, and a Spanish general of artillery. Opposite me sit a high official of the navy ministry and some count or other. I know them all well by now, sit down in my place, greeting them on all sides, because I am in a peculiar mood I say not another word until the goodbye with which I take my leave. Then I am alone on the street and really can't see what purpose this evening served. I go home and regret that I didn't marry. Naturally this mood passes away again, whether because I have thought it through to the end, whether because the thoughts have dispersed. But on occasion it comes back again. (*D* 208–9)

Despite a general sense of the absurdity of life, Loewy is still proud of his status symbols, of his obvious wealth and of the high society in which he moves. Kafka the clever diarist purposely ends the interior monologue, which he is obviously quoting freely from memory, with Loewy's inability and reluctance to come to grips with the true reason for his recurring dissatisfaction, not to say unhappiness.

There was no lack of recognition or honours for Loewy in his position as Director of the railway. The Spanish government decorated him; and at the end of October 1905 he and three other prominent members of the French colony in Madrid were named Chevaliers of the Légion d'honneur by the President of France, Émile Loubet, who was on a state visit to Spain.[8] The decoration was a reward not only for Loewy's part in the creation of a smooth-running railway but also for his support of French interests abroad.

All in all, 1905 proved a very good year for the railway Director. The high point came when he travelled to Washington DC to attend the Seventh International Railway Congress. On 13 May the President of the United States, Theodore Roosevelt, received the delegates to the congress in the garden of the White House. Standing on a Persian carpet spread out on the lawn under the shade of the giant trees, the President – as one newspaper reported – welcomed each participant with a hearty handshake, while a Marine band played in the background.[9] Loewy took the opportunity to transmit his patron's best wishes to the man whose gunboat diplomacy had given cover to Bunau-Varilla's intrigues in Panama only a short time before, machinations which had included his appointment as plenipotentiary of the newly founded republic so that he could at once sign away the canal rights, for a pittance, to the United States in perpetuity.

Roosevelt remembered Varilla well. 'When I uttered your name,' Loewy wrote to Bunau-Varilla in Paris on the day of the reception, 'Mr Roosevelt's face assumed an expression of true pleasure; he advanced a pace towards me, grasped my hand heartily and said, "Mr Bunau-Varilla is a great man. What he has done for Panama is extraordinary. I congratulate you on having been in Panama with him and am especially happy to be able to shake your hand."'[10] It can safely be assumed that this description of the meeting with the President of the United States was repeated to the family in Prague. It might have given Kafka the inspiration years later to write of the President's theatre box in the last chapter of *Amerika*. Characteristically, Karl Rossman gets to see the President's box only in a picture, that is, at second hand.

Alfred remained in close contact with his family at home. Kafka's diaries and letters refer to a number of visits, but there may have been others which were not so recorded, especially before 1910 when Alfred's father and stepmother were still alive. (Julie died in 1908, Jakob in 1910.) From the diary one also learns that Kafka and his uncle corresponded, if only sporadically. It seems likely that their letters often dealt with the young man's future – or so one may infer from what he wrote to Felice on 28 February/1 March 1913. Two weeks before, he had sent her one of his uncle's letters to read; now he said, 'The other day in connection with my uncle's letter you asked me about my plans and prospects' (*LF* 209). Questions of this kind, questions which not only demanded information but also challenged him to show some ambition, were extremely irritating for Kafka. In this case at least he answered with impatience and petulance that he could do no more than crash or grind or stumble into the future, and indeed would prefer to lie still in the present.

His feelings towards his relative in Madrid are clearly ambivalent. In the critical summer of 1913, following a reproach by his mother that his uncle deserved a letter in reply – 'He has telegraphed, he has written, he has your welfare so much at heart' – Kafka was ready with a curt response: 'These are simply formalities, he is a complete stranger to me, he misunderstands me entirely, he does not know what I want and need, I have nothing in common with him' (*D* 228). Yet at much the same time (5 August 1913) he described Uncle Alfred as his 'closest relative, much closer to me than my parents', and he had told him of his impending engagement several weeks before he told his parents (*LF* 297). In his letter to the newly engaged couple, Loewy for his part – addressing himself more to the young woman – writes of 'our Franz, who is critical of certain things in me', indicating that the relationship between uncle and nephew was close enough to allow the open expression of criticism (*LF* 413). Diffidently Alfred goes on to reassure Felice: 'Not that I blame him, for I am not without faults'.

When Kafka's youngest sister was preparing for her wedding in 1920, he asked her in a letter whether Alfred was coming and, when she did not reply, asked her again, plainly anxious to see him once more after the long separation brought about by the World War.[11] It is most likely that it was in July 1920 that Loewy and his relatives in Prague were together for the last time. On 28 February 1923, he died in Madrid of renal sclerosis and was buried in that city's Catholic Cementerio de la Sacramental de Santa Maria. His fortune of 600,000 Czech crowns – or, as Kafka said, what was left of this fortune after the French and Spanish governments as well as Madrid and Parisian lawyers had gobbled up their share – was divided among his sister Julie and his brothers Joseph, Richard and Siegfried (*L* 393).

The director of the railway company and other officials celebrating the bridging of a river on the Matadi–Stanley Pool line, 1890s

5

Kalda Railway, Kafka Railway, Loewy Railway: The Loewys in the Work of Franz Kafka

Franz Kafka himself remarked in a letter to Felice Bauer of 5 August 1913 how much he had let his uncle in Madrid influence him in his first major work. 'There is undoubtedly a great deal of my uncle in "The Judgement",' he wrote, '(he is a bachelor, director of railways in Madrid, knows the whole of Europe *with the exception of Russia*) . . .' (*LF* 297). 'The Judgement' was written seventeen days after Loewy's confession to his nephew, described in the last chapter, that his life was somewhat unsatisfying. Kafka draws on Loewy's lifestyle for the character of Georg Bendemann's friend in Russia, who has no real relationships in the expatriate colony in St Petersburg nor among indigenous Russian families, and has resigned himself to permanent bachelorhood (*IPS* 45).

Joseph Loewy's Congo experiences have already been mentioned as the starting-point for the Congo Railway fragment in the octavo notebook of 1917. Indeed his influence is discernible in an earlier fragment in the same notebook, which begins with the question, 'You know the Trocadéro in Paris?' and goes on to deal with a great trial which is taking place in the building (*W* 58). Were not the models for this big trial those other very real trials in the French capital, Panama and Dreyfus? It is perhaps no coincidence that Kafka chose the name Trocadéro, for at the time of his arrest Captain Dreyfus lived at number 6 avenue de Trocadéro, which was also the street in which the offices of Maurice Bunau-Varilla's *Le Matin* were located.[1] Showing his nephew around Paris, Joseph might well have pointed out the building which housed the enterprise of the family to whom he owed so much.

But the text in which the influence of both Loewys is undeniable is the long fragment 'Memoirs of the Kalda Railway', which Kafka began in August 1914. His employer, the Workers' Accident Insurance Institute, had granted him several extra weeks in addition to his normal holiday, and he used the free time to write, apparently working on several texts at the same time, but primarily on the novel *The Trial* and the 'Kalda Railway' story (*D* 324). The figure of the uncle, distorted into the ridiculous, dominates a whole chapter in the novel. These characteristics can perhaps be traced to more than one model. The fact that K.'s uncle lives in the country points to the country doctor Siegfried Loewy, the youngest of Julie Kafka's four brothers. But in the opening scenes the author equipped the elderly relative from the country with a panama hat, a small reminder of the exotic Loewys abroad (*T* 103). One think also of K.'s position in the bank as chief clerk, *Prokurist* in German, which comes very close to the French *fondé de pouvoirs* used by Alfred Loewy to describe the job he held in the bank of the Bunau-Varillas in Paris. The protagonist's first name, Joseph, might also have been borrowed from Joseph Loewy.

But the lives of the Loewys are of much greater importance for the railway story, which in its turn must be seen in conjunction with the composition of *The Trial*. 'Kalda' of course reminds one in the first place of 'Kafka', into which the 'l' of 'Loewy' has crept. There is clearly a hint of the German adjective *kalt* (cold) and the story is about coldness: the coldness of the Russian climate and the coldness that results from lack of contact with human beings. The final 'a' in Kalda can also be found in the names of some places in the Congo, such as Palaballa, the steep mountain incline which had to be overcome by the railway

View of the specially constructed dining hall at Tumba prepared for the inauguration banquet on 3 July 1896

engineers, and the important clolonial settlements of Boma and Tumba – the latter being the halfway station of the Congo Railway where Thys held the banquet for the senior administrative personnel of the Compagnie du Chemin de Fer du Congo, among them Joseph Loewy. Accounts of this event and mention of other places important in the Belgian Congo's early colonial history could well have come to the ears of the adventurous young Kafka in the 1890s either through Joseph himself, on leave in Prague, or through Alfred, who was always well informed of his brother's life and movements.

Obviously Kafka was thinking of his expatriate uncle in the days before he began writing the 'Kalda Railway' story. On 11 August 1914, Kafka writes in his diary about a daydream 'that I have remained in Paris, walk through it arm in arm with my uncle, pressed close to his side' (*D* 303). An incident in the railway story, which seems unconnected with the rest, becomes significant when seen as the author's comment on the source of his fiction: from time to time an

Views of the Congo railway from the 1890s showing the steep inclines and narrow gorges the engineers were faced with

old newspaper is thrown out from a passing train to the narrator in his station hut. It contains 'the gossip [literally: scandal stories – *Skandalgeschichten*] of Kalda, which would have interested me but which I could not understand from disconnected issues' (D 309). Is Kafka alluding to the Panama *affaire* and at the same time to his encoding of his allusion into a 'disconnected' [*einzelnen*] sentence?

After a few short introductory sentences the first-person narrator of the 'memoirs of the Kalda Railway' launches into a description of the railway venture in which he was employed years before. He stresses the economic aspects of the railway: 'the little railway may originally have been built with some commercial purpose in view, but the capital had been insufficient, construction came to a halt, and instead of terminating at Kalda, the nearest village of any size, a five days' journey from us by wagon, the railway came to an end at a small settlement right in the wilderness . . .' (D 303–5). The ill-conceived railway runs trains only twice a day, transporting light loads of goods and a few field hands in summer. In many respects this matches the description of the Congo Railway, at one stage of its development at least. Because of the difficult terrain between Matadi and Stanley Pool it had been possible to lay only a narrow-gauge line. In the photographs that have survived the locomotives look more like toy trains than serious means of transport. The construction of the Congo Railway did indeed come to a virtual standstill at time during the first difficult years and the flow of capital was interrupted for periods before 1895. The tracks ended in the wasteland of the Congolese bush.[2] But Kafka depicts this desperate interim stage as a permanent and hopeless condition. Given this precarious state of affairs the narrator's means of support are of course constantly in jeopardy. Obviously, the economic goals of the Compagnie du Chemin de Fer du Congo had been much more precisely defined, though they may not have seemed so to outsiders. The unstable financial circumstances of the Kalda Railway also mirror the continual financial plight of Alfred Loewy's Spanish railway, which Kafka must surely have known about.

Kafka seems to have fashioned other characteristics in his story directly in contrast to conditions in the Congo. A varied landscape with tropical rain forest, mountains, rivers, ravines and high plateaux has been transformed into a monotonously flat Russian steppe. There is hardly a tree to obstruct the view far into the distance. The brutal heat of the Congo becomes a cold climate in Kafka's story. (Perhaps some aspects of the landscape and climate which Joseph Loewy encountered in China have crept in here.) Certainly the small wooden shed, left behind from the days of construction, which serves as a railway station and makeshift home for the narrator, calls to mind the crude huts which, as already mentioned, were used by the agents of the Congo Railway and which feature in Kafka's octavo notebook. The hut is primitively furnished, and in all other respects life is hard. Food and other necessities of life are in particularly inadequate supply: the few provisions delivered by the railway company are not fit for consumption.

But these are outward characteristics which Kafka gathered from the life of his uncle Joseph and worked into his tale. There are further similarities which reach into the very kernel of the story. It tells of subordination, well known to Kafka from the lives of both his uncles, but especially from Alfred Loewy's: the subordination to a sense of duty, magnified by fear. The irony in the narrator's situation, also present in Joseph Loewy's life in the Congo and obviously the inspiration of this theme, is this: the train, built as a means of transport from place to place, comes out of the distance (from the narrator's point of view) and disappears again into the distance. He, however, is bound to his post and dares not remove himself too far from his miserable little station shed in case he lose his job. His uncle's life, glamorous as it might have seemed to the young Kafka, is reduced to watching and waiting for trains he cannot use to escape this desolate life. It reflects the inner bondage the author himself felt in his job at the Workers' Accident Insurance Institute. Only when he leaves his shed to clean and inspect the rails does the narrator stray further than the prescribed distance of one kilometre on either side of his station. The many black dots he sees in the distance, which he takes for approaching troops, are not only an optical illusion but stem from his bad conscience at having transgressed the regulations of his job. And should someone indeed arrive at the station, he hurries to return to his post, his freedom of movement obviously limited by his sense of duty to railway regulations, which stop him from indulging his urge to get away.

Even in this lonely foreign post the authoritarian structure of the railway administration makes itself felt, bringing home the reality of economic dependency. Once a month the record book and the revenues of the station master are checked, a task reminiscent of Joseph Loewy's bookkeeping job. The inspector tries to intimidate his employee by browbeating, by suspiciously checking the daybook and in the end by threatening the total collapse of the railway and the loss of his job. In this way the inspector emphasizes the great chasm between their social positions. But after the audit both men get drunk and the difference in rank between them quickly melts away. The two of them are now joined in the brotherhood of the economically oppressed, and together they curse the railway administration. Finally the drunken debauch ends in an embrace that lasts all night. The inspector initiates this homoerotic scene by promising a splendid career to the narrator.

Nothing mirrors the poverty of human relations more than this relationship of inspector to narrator: first the brutal attempt to stress subordination, then the false fraternization in a drunken orgy. A few years later Kafka depicted an even more crass example of this relationship in 'A Report to an Academy', when the ape Rotpeter, on the boat bringing him to civilization, has to learn from the sailors how to drink before he can be accepted as a member of the human race (*IPS* 179).

But it is possible that the primitive debauch in Kafka's 'Kalda Railway' story has a more concrete origin. Congo expert René J. Cornet reported that, although drunkenness was a problem, for some it was the only way to deal with the intolerable conditions. Punishment for drunkenness among blacks and whites was routine in the Congo. During an inspection trip carried out by the Director Albert Thys in September 1890 some engineers employed in the construction of the railway banded together to compose an ironic letter to ask why wines and spirits were being denied them.[3] Surely Loewy heard of this when he arrived in the Congo early the next year. In Kafka's 'Memoirs of the Kalda Railway', the travelling inspector carries a large store of drink with him while the narrator has to content himself with the dregs, which he guzzles down after his superior has left. For the rest of the month he remains sober.

The link between the narrator and the inhabitants of the area is superficial. Although he reports at first that they were not put off from visiting him by the distance they had to travel, he recognizes right away that 'they came only on the chance of transacting some business with me, nor did they make any attempt to conceal their purpose' (*D* 306). As in the Congo, traffic with the 'natives' is limited to the exchange of goods. No genuine relationship develops out of this trade; on the contrary, the indigenous people despise him because of his buying their wares.

It is notable that in his 'Kalda Railway' story Kafka returned to his use of Russia as a metaphor, first employed in 'The Judgement', embellishing it with further detail taken from the lives of his two uncles. This metaphor describes the void into which Kafka himself had fled in the summer of 1914 after breaking off his engagement to Felice Bauer. He was alone again, cut off from the people around him, bound to the routine of his job. He had also failed in all his diversionary activities, just as the narrator fails in his attempts at gardening or at hunting wild animals (he finds out that there are none in this desolate wilderness).

But on closer scrutiny the reader makes the astonishing discovery that Kafka, for all the desolation he depicted in the fragment, clearly intended to write a positive story, a counterpart to his novel *The Trial*. In his diary he also made the point that he allowed himself to write the 'Russian' story only after *The Trial* (D 313). Right at the beginning, the narrator emphatically separates the present from the past by saying, 'During one period in my life – it is many years ago now –' (D 303). The word 'memoirs' in the title of the story likewise stresses that it is the distant past which is being chronicled. (The temporal perspective of the narrator's railway experiences, incidentally, is the same as Joseph Loewy's, for by 1914 his Congo adventures were also many years in the past.) The explicit reference to the past points to an epoch that has been completed and digested. The former refugee from humanity has presumably either returned from the deserted steppe or come to terms with living there (or in even greater loneliness). He concedes that such a lonely life has the power to disperse his cares, yet at the same time he admits that he 'was not particularly suited to stand a condition of utter solitude', and in a general reflection – the only one to be found in this story – he comes to a conclusion most extraordinary for Kafka: 'Solitude is powerful beyond everything else, and drives one back to people' (D 305–6).

This fragmentary story offers no explanation of how the narrator saves himself. Would he, like Joseph Loewy, take his place in human society after years in the wilderness, and perhaps even marry? When Kafka began 'Memoirs of the Kalda Railway' and *The Trial*, he had just broken off his engagement to Felice. The novel settled accounts with his past life and the events that had led to the break with his fiancée. In it he depicts Joseph K.'s cheerless, empty life, devoid of true human contact. In his 'Kalda Railway' story, in which the narrator has survived to look back on his life, he obviously wanted to portray victory over such loneliness.

Postcards of Chicago and New York from Alfred Loewy to his parents in Prague, 1905

6

The Discovery of the New World:
Kafka's American Cousins and Amerika

The two Loewy brothers were able to tell their family about their experiences in North America, both having been there for short visits to different places at different times. Kafka gave Karl Rossmann, the hero of his novel *Der Verschollene* (*The Missing Person*, given the title *Amerika* by Max Brod), a rich uncle in New York. Seen against the backdrop of family members who served as sources for the novel, it appears ironic when – after handing Karl the letter from his uncle banning him from his household – the sly Mr Green remarks with malicious pleasure, 'I bet you haven't a second uncle in America' (*A* 104). Karl could have answered, of course, that although just then he did not have a second uncle he did have a whole series of cousins, for apart from the two Loewy brothers there were a number of representatives of the *mishpocheh* of Kafka's generation who had emigrated to the United States. The novel is based on particulars of their lives.

'As Karl Rossmann, a poor boy of sixteen who had been packed off to America by his parents because a servant girl had seduced him and got herself with child by him, stood on the liner slowly entering the harbour of New York, a sudden burst of sunshine seemed to illumine the Statue of Liberty, so that he saw it in a new light, although he had sighted it long before' (*A* 13). Already in the first sentence of the novel there is a reworking of real events. According to a

Otto Kafka

report from one member of the family, Robert Kafka, the author's cousin from the small Bohemian town of Kolin, had been seduced by the family cook, who had made him a father at the tender age of fourteen.[1] Consciously or unconsciously, Franz Kafka seems to have used elements of his cousin's name in that of his protagonist, by taking the first two letters of the first and last name and placing the two letter groups in reverse order: *Ro*bert *Ka*fka/*Ka*rl *Ro*ssmann. When choosing Klara Pollunder as the name for the spoiled daughter of the rich New York businessman Rossmann visits, Kafka probably had the name of Robert's mother in mind: *Klara Poláček*.

The most outstanding of Kafka's American cousins was Otto Kafka (1879–1939), the eldest son of the merchant Filip Kafka from Kolin. He went to school in his home town, but with no more than average success,[2] and attended the Commercial College in Prague and the Exportakademie in Vienna. His temperament, energetic by all accounts, could not endure the confines of the small backwater community in Bohemia. He is believed to have run away to Paris at an early age because he saw no future for himself in the family business. Indeed, an entry in the Registry of Issued Passports and Visas 1890/1 to 1898 at the Austrian Consulate indicates that Otto applied for a passport there at the age of seventeen or eighteen.[3] He then apparently boarded a ship bound for Buenos Aires. The young man's flight from home and his sojourn in foreign lands might well have inspired Franz Kafka's boyhood attempt to write a novel about two brothers, one of whom emigrates to America while the other is in prison in Europe, a work the author later described in his diary (*D* 37).

Argentina did not hold the restless adventurer for long. For several years he wandered around in the world, returned home after one or two years in South America, moved out to South Africa for a while, then, after completing his military service at home, returned to Buenos Aires in 1904, where he applied for a position at the Austro-Hungarian Consulate. He was unsuccessful, so he entered into partnership with a man named Schlesinger. While Otto was on a business trip to his native country, Schlesinger took the opportunity to liquidate the firm and abscond with all the capital. One version of the story has it that, without means, Otto was forced to work his way to North America as a steward on a ship. A passenger list records his landing in New York on board the liner *Pennsylvania* (Hamburg America Line) in May 1906, but only as a 'non-immigrant alien' in transit to Buenos Aires.[4] It must be assumed that he either changed his mind and remained in the United States in May or that he indeed left and returned later the same year via another port for which no records were kept. There are other clues that suggest the latter course of events might have taken place.

On 11 December 1906 Franz Kafka wrote to his friend Max Brod about his 'interesting cousin from Paraguay', who was passing through Prague and could stay only one night. He had spoken to Brod of his cousin and he wanted to show him to his friend (*L* 22). The 'interesting' cousin was most likely Otto Kafka, who seems to have returned to Europe on a quick visit. The author's eagerness to bring his cousin and Brod together bears witness to the impression Otto had made on him.

There were others, apart from Franz Kafka, who were keen to contact Otto Kafka: on 13 September 1906 the circuit court at Jičín in northern Bohemia had issued a warrant for his arrest on 'suspicion of fraud by eliciting wares from the Count Harrach Glass Factory in Neuwelt to the value of over 600 crowns and cash amounting to 250 crowns; he [Kafka] was formerly representative of that firm in America'.[5] All the country's court and police officials were directed to take him into custody as soon as he set foot on Austrian soil and to deliver him up to the court. The fact that this warrant was not reissued and that Otto was not arrested when he returned to Bohemia later indicates that it was based on a misapprehension. Perhaps it was the result of the staggering debts incurred when Otto was bankrupted by his dishonest partner in South America and which he found impossible to pay off immediately. The hard-hearted manu-facturer preferred to treat it as fraud. In any case, this affair had an effect on Kafka, who must have known of the true circumstances. One of the chief components of *Amerika* is Karl Rossmann's flight from a stern, unyielding system of law enforcement pursuing him for little or no reason.

Otto Kafka's beginnings in the United States certainly resemble those of Kafka's protagonist. In 1918, when he was unjustly detained on suspicion of spying for the enemy, Otto wrote the following description of his first period in the New World in a petition to the Assistant Attorney-General:

During the twelve years since I landed in this country, as ever before, I relied upon nobody's support or assistance. I did not make a single penny except by hard work and I have tried my best to adapt myself as quickly as possible to American views and ideals. When I arrived I did not know a soul. I had no means and could not speak the language. I started as a porter with a corset concern at $5 a week and worked myself up to be-come manager of an export department that I created, overcoming con-siderable opposition on part of the heads of the concern. The formerly reluctant head of the company became soon very interested in the new departure, when results began to show.
I stayed there for three years and left because of intrigues of my assistant against me while on a trip abroad.[6]

Alone, without money, unable to speak English – there is no doubt of the similarity with Karl Rossmann upon his arrival in New York.

Of course, Otto's later career suggests that of Rossmann's rich uncle, Senator Edward Jakob, who has built up a gigantic enterprise out of a little business near the docks (*A* 59). When Franz Kafka began his first and second versions of the novel in 1911–12, Otto's star was beginning to ascend

Page of autograph manuscript of *Amerika*

once again. In 1911 he founded an export firm, the Distributing Corporation, with its head office in New York City, and in March of the same year had married an American, Alice Stickney.[7] The Stickneys were an old American family, several of whose members had been politicians and statesmen. Knowledge of this might have prompted Kafka to give Rossmann's uncle the title of senator and to set part of the story in the upper strata of New York society.

It should not be forgotten that Kafka's two maternal uncles, Joseph and Alfred Loewy, who had been in North America had lived at the upper end of the social scale. By choosing the name Jakob for the Senator, Franz Kafka was pointing to the two sources for his novel, the Kafkas and the Löwys, for it was the name his two grandfathers had shared. He even emphasizes the point when Rossmann explains that he was not at first able to recognize his uncle by name, and this turns out to be because in his new home Jakob had used his given name as his surname (*A* 36). So it is highly ironical – Kafka's private joke – when Senator Jakob issues the invitation, 'And now I want you to tell me candidly whether I am your uncle or not' (*A* 40). Further proof of the novel's debt to at least one set of grandparents is the photograph of Karl's parents which he has brought with him and which – as other scholars have noticed – was modelled on the photograph of the writer's grandparents Jakob and Franziska Kafka.

Moreover, in the first chapter Kafka at once addresses this very question of the transformation of fact into fiction. After Senator Jakob has recounted the story of Karl's seduction to the people assembled in the purser's office and Karl has himself privately relived the scenes with the servant-girl, he says to his uncle, 'you're mistaken if you think my father and mother never speak kindly of you. In any case, you've got some points quite wrong in your story; I mean that it didn't all happen like that in reality' (*A* 41). One may treat this statement by Karl as Kafka's oblique admission that he has rewritten the stories of his relatives in his own fashion, and somewhat indiscreetly, to further the aims of his fiction. And, as if to give them redress, he has placed their protests in the mouth of his young protagonist.

Particulars of Otto Kafka's life and aspects of his personality may be discernible in the character of Senator Edward Jakob. In the novel he moves with great resolution towards any goal he has set himself. Nothing seems to deter him from carrying out a plan once he has determined on it. According to reports, and his own actions demonstrate this, Otto Kafka possessed similar traits. He pursued his goals with great energy and did not shy away from acting decisively to secure his rights. Evidence of this is given by newspaper reports of measures he took in 1918 to sue for breach of contract his business partner, the influential financier General Coleman T. Dupont (a former Postmaster-General and member of the famed Dupont chemical family) – a daunting undertaking in those days when such people were regarded with awe. Similarly he tried to have the Mexican Finance Minister, Adolfo de la Huerta, served with a court order when he paid an official visit to New York in June 1922, and force him to honour a contract the Mexican government had concluded with Kafka concerning steel for railways. All in all, Otto Kafka was a no-nonsense type. 'One must learn to obey before one commands' was apparently one of his favourite sayings.[8]

Some of the traits of Otto's wife Alice seem to have gone – albeit in exaggerated form – into the figure of Klara

Pollunder. Little of her outward appearance is given beyond her red lips and the 'brilliance of her lively eyes' (*A* 73). A good deal more of her personality becomes apparent in the short time she is with Rossmann. Although there are indications of softer, more passive elements in her nature, episodes like the wrestling match in which she overcomes Karl with a few well-practised ju-jitsu holds stamp her character for us. Kafka emphasizes the Amazon in Klara. Her 'athletic' body is obviously strong enough to lift her guest into the air (*A* 77). Nor does she make any attempt to restrain her sharp tongue.

Alice Stickney certainly provided Franz Kafka with a model for Klara Pollunder (though, as with Otto, the author was very eclectic, taking only certain aspects). She was by all accounts a very determined and independent woman.[9] Born in the American Midwest, in Chippewa Falls, Wisconsin, she is said to have done social work on an Indian reservation before going to Chicago to study art. Around 1908–9 she moved to New York City, where she took up residence as a painter and illustrator in the artists' quarter of Greenwich Village. She was a student of Robert Henri, founder of the so-called Ashcan School of painting, who encouraged self-expression in his disciples. How did Franz Kafka learn the details of his cousin Otto's life in America or of Alice's temperament? According to Otto's testimony given during interrogation in 1918, he wrote letters to his family in Kolin until 1915 when the war interrupted the correspondence. His father Filip, so it seems, was very proud of his relatives in America, and carried photographs of them around with him which he liked to show to everyone, no doubt adding glowing reports. But one event is crucial: in the late autumn of 1911, at a very critical phase of Kafka's work on his novel, Otto, his wife and new-born son were in Europe. Otto apparently took the opportunity to bring his wife to Kolin to introduce her to his family.

During his time in America Otto Kafka never admitted his relationship to his cousin the writer (whose fame, when Otto died in 1939, was far from secure). One family member reports that in later years Alice claimed to have met Franz Kafka. But though it is doubtful whether they were personally acquainted, we can be sure that the vivacious young American's visit to Kolin did not go unnoticed among the wider circle of relatives, especially since she did not refrain from conversational sparring with her father-in-law. When the latter complained that American women were not family-minded because they did not want many children, if any, Alice is supposed to have countered that she would prove the opposite by giving birth to six children, the very number that he had fathered. (She did.)

A further primary source for Kafka's novel was Otto's younger brother Franz, or Frank as he was known in America, who arrived in New York on the *Pennsylvania* in June 1909.[10] Frank (1893–1953), like Karl Rossmann, was only sixteen when he emigrated. That they had the same name must have aroused strange feelings in the author. Here was a young man, his namesake, who had achieved what he had not: the break with home. Frank had attended school in Kolin for four years and a commercial college for one. In 1910–11, after his arrival in the New World, his brother sent him to a private school, the Irving Preparatory School in Tarrytown, not far from New York City. Tarrytown had become renowned in the mid-nineteenth century through the author Washington Irving, who had built his villa Sunnyside there, as well as providing the name of the school. It had some reputation as an exclusive resort, since the celebrated millionaires Jay Gould and John D. Rockefeller owned large estates there.

Otto too must have been struck by the attractive location; several years later, when he had made his fortune, he bought an estate there near the Rockefellers'. No doubt reports of the town where Frank had spent a year at school, and possibly descriptions of the school itself, made their way back to Kolin and further; probably the illustrious Rockefeller family was also mentioned. Out of this ambience came the chapter in Kafka's *Amerika* entitled 'A Country House Near New York'. Karl Rossmann is invited to the newly renovated house of rich businessman Mr Pollunder, some distance by car from the city. It is telling that the author does not provide a detailed description of the house – he arrives as dusk is falling and its outlines recede into the dark. It has been pointed out that everything in the novel is seen from the perspective of the protagonist, who at this point in the story knows only the houses in his uncle's street. Thus the observation (from Karl's point of view) that the structure, 'like the country houses of most rich people in the neighbourhood of New York, was larger and taller than a country house ... has any need to be' (*A* 66) remains perplexing. How is he to know what the usual type of country house looks like? Is this proof of an omniscient, authorial narrator or does the deliberate (or unconscious) break in perspective represent a subtle indication that this comment must be seen as coming from the real author standing outside the fictional framework?

Karl's dim perception of his physical surroundings includes the interior of the house. Electricity has not been installed yet and he is forced to rely on the small circle of light provided by a candle. Whatever else this scene may suggest, it can be seen as another ironic comment by the author on his use of borrowed facts. He has cleverly projected his own uncertainty on to his protagonist, who gropes in the dark. Karl's impression of the house derives more from what he senses than from what he actually sees.

After his schooling in Tarrytown Frank entered his brother's business as a clerk and even spent a short time in a subsidiary in Havana, Cuba.[11] No sudden change of fortune like Rossmann's banishment from his family occurred. But Otto, on whom Frank depended during the first years, experienced fluctuating fortunes, and there the background of Rossmann's fall from grace can be found. Nineteen-twelve, the year after his visit to Kolin, brought hard times: Otto's partner, Jacob Brandon, forced his resignation from the firm he had founded. Again completely without means, he had to borrow – in his own words – one hundred dollars here, fifty dollars there, until he had collected enough capital to start the Kafka Export Company. (On a rainy night in February 1913 he and his family once more found themselves on the street.)[12]

On 9 December 1914, Kafka writes in his diary about a visit of 'E.K.' from Chicago, and notes several points about the latter's description of his 'placid life' – his work in a

Above: Emil and Elsa Kafka on a visit to Leitmeritz in 1926; below Emil Kafka's certificate of naturalization, 1911; above right: Max Kohn, Karoline (Fleischer) Kohn and her husband Sigmund in the 20s

mail-order house, the way he spent his free time, some of his opinions about life in America (*D* 320). 'E.K.' was yet another cousin, Emil Kafka (1881–1963), the son of his uncle Heinrich Kafka. The father was a merchant in the northern Bohemian town of Leitmeritz, who had died suddenly at the age of thirty-six in 1886. Emil had already emigrated to the United States in 1904, because he, like Otto, saw no prospect of a career in the family business.[13] His mother Karoline (née Fleischner) had married Sigmund Kohn, the manager of a shop, and seemed to have favoured the children of this marriage. Emil's elder brother Viktor (1880–1915) followed Emil to Chicago. Both lived there with a rich uncle, Max Kohn, who owned a department store in the city, but who kept such a close watch on their daily activities that they both moved out.[14] Viktor soon returned to his native country; Emil found work at first with a local dry-goods firm, Eisinger, Dessauer & Co., then with the burgeoning and already well-known mail-order business Sears, Roebuck & Co.

Some aspects of Senator Jakob's business show a striking similarity to the gigantic Chicago firm, certainly the halls of telegraphs and telephones in the second chapter of *Amerika*, rooms of huge dimensions, larger than the telegraph office in Karl's home town. In the Senator's offices, uninterrupted contact is maintained with clients and great store is set by the short but precise messages that are speedily transmitted

Photographs from 'A Visit to Sears Roebuch & Co.'; above: the Scribing Department; above right: Index and Rating; below: the Entry Department

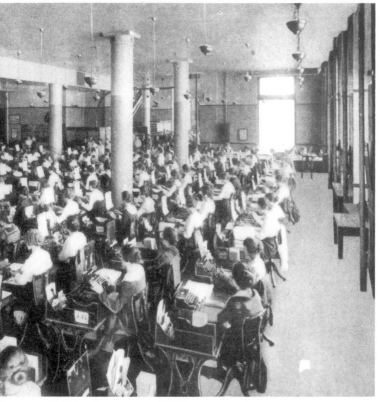

Herrmann Kafka (?)

to other departments. The incessant traffic of 'people rushing hither and thither', who have no time to exchange greetings, smacks of a Chaplinesque assembly line (*A* 59). At Sears there was a series of similar rooms, where incoming orders were opened, sorted and processed. Brochures with many photographs such as *A Visit to Sears, Roebuck & Co.* were circulated to provide the public with an impressive introduction to the size and uniqueness of the firm. These publicity pamphlets stressed the large volume and great speed of business: 90,000 to 180,000 letters delivered daily, 450 envelopes opened by machine per minute, all incoming letters answered within twenty-four hours. Photographs showed large halls with 300, 400 or even 500 employees sorting, dictating or typing letters.

Emil Kafka seems to have been very taken with Sears and all things American, and tried to pass his enthusiasm on to others. (His American profligacy in throwing away wrapping paper, string and nails caused great consternation in the

Heinrich Kafka

family shop at home.) Descriptions of the huge firm that employed him in the United States reached his family (and through them Kafka and the relatives in Prague) even before his return to Leitmeritz in 1914. Since he still enjoyed leafing through old Sears catalogues years later when back in his European home, we may be sure that he sent them and other publicity publications such as the above-mentioned brochures back to his relatives as soon as he began working at the mail-order house. The scene set in the buffet bar of the Hotel Occidental in the novel's fourth chapter (*A* 126–9) could have originated in Emil's tales, for he apparently liked to tell of the saloons in Chicago where for the price of a glass of beer one could help oneself at the buffet to all the food one wanted.

Photographs play no small role in Franz Kafka's life and they figure in *Amerika* too. In the fifth chapter Karl finds himself in the living-room of the hotel's head cook and has a look at some framed photographs standing on a small sideboard. As mentioned before, it has been pointed out that one of them resembles a photograph of Franz Kafka's grandparents. But it has yet to be revealed that another one derives from a photograph from Emil Kafka's family: Rossmann's attention is caught by a picture of a young soldier 'who had laid his cap on a table and was standing erect with a thatch of wild, black hair and a look of suppressed but arrogant amusement' (*A* 147). This is similar to a portrait of Heinrich Kafka, Emil's father, taken during his military service.[15] (A photograph album in the possession of Heinrich Kafka's son Rudolf contained pictures of Hermann Kafka and his family; it can be conjectured that albums in Franz Kafka's family also carried photographs of the wider *mishpocheh*.)

Finally, in the seventh chapter, entitled 'A Refuge', there is one more reminder of Emil Kafka. Between two and three o'clock in the morning Karl finds himself on the balcony of Brunelda's apartment speaking to a student on a neighbouring balcony who studies by night and works during the day as a salesman in Montly's department store for a paltry salary (*A* 278). The term *Warenhaus* (department store) again suggests a large business like Sears, Roebuck, although the name Montly sounds more like the name of another large Chicago mail-order firm, Montgomery Ward. Before he became a US citizen, Emil attended a preparatory course for candidates for citizenship. His acquisition of citizenship in October 1911 could have given impetus to the novel, the first version of which must have been started at this time (Kafka later destroyed it). One can easily date this balcony scene and connect it with the relatives in Leitmeritz. Immediately after completing it during the night of 5/6 January 1913, Kafka wrote to Felice, 'At this moment two people – grown somewhat dim since yesterday – are talking to each other on two adjacent balconies on the eighth floor at three o'clock in the morning' (*LF* 142). Three had a half weeks before, Kafka had visited Emil's family in Leitmeritz (*LF* 96).

These numerous details leave no doubt that the lives of the American cousins served as sources for certain aspects of *Amerika*. But one should not forget that fundamental to the novel is their emigration to the New World. Otto, Frank and Emil left home at early age and found worldly success, unlike Karl Rossmann. Kafka did not just take the idea of emigration literally as a plot device; he saw it as a metaphor for the child's passage into the adult world, a world in which Kafka was never comfortable. Karl's uncle likens European's first days in America to an earlier stage in life: he compares the arrival to birth (*A* 50). One recalls that Karl Rossmann's passage into the new world of adulthood is precipitated by his seduction and a sexual encounter which he does not comprehend but which results in the birth of a child. Becoming a father, which Kafka considered the high point of a man's life, but which he himself despaired of achieving, is thrust upon Rossmann without his having understood, much less enjoyed, sexuality. Despite his innocence he is considered guilty and expelled from the world of his childhood.

Kafka also places Karl's hour of triumph in the new country in the first chapter, when he comes to the aid of the stoker trying to defend himself before a 'tribunal' in the purser's office. With the awakening of social conscience, independence begins to manifest itself – two very positive elements in the passage from childhood to adulthood. Of course, as soon as he falls into the clutches of his business-minded uncle, his freedom of movement is curtailed, his motivation is dampened. Here one is reminded again of Alfred Loewy, a living example of someone within high society who had to conform to the wishes of his master. Kafka's cousins became acclimatized and blossomed in the New World, so they could justly boast of their successes or speak 'almost touchingly' of their 'placid life'. Rossmann, on the other hand, as the novel progresses becomes increasingly unsure, confused and in a way 'younger' during his sojourn in America. German literature has greatly valued the so-called novel of development (*Entwicklungsroman*), which even in its most primitive form shows the protagonist reaching ever higher plateaux of insight and wisdom through experience. Kafka too writes a novel of development but has typically and cleverly transformed the ascending into a descending line, development into regression.

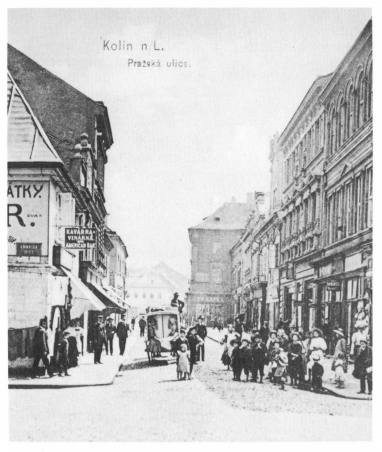

Detail of a postcard of Kolin dating from the beginning of the century showing Prague Street with Filip Kafka's shop at the bottom of the street on the right

7

The Mishpocheh *That Stayed at Home: Czechs, Germans, Jews, Assimilated Jews*

By emigrating, some Löwys and Kafkas were trying to flee their gloomy future and make a career elsewhere. The previous chapters have described their successes and the difficulties they encountered. Of the many relatives of the older generation who stayed at home in Bohemia, all without exception were able to escape the impoverished rural surroundings in which they had grown up. All to a certain extent 'made it'. Such exodus from the 'ghetto-like little village community', as Kafka characterized it (*W* 194), into the city usually heralded the first stages of the assimilation process. This did not necessarily lead to conversion and the complete abandonment of Judaism, more likely to a benign neglect of the old religious rites and rules. Kafka himself expressed the regret to his father that he had not been brought up in stricter religious observance (*W* 192). It was left to other members of the younger generation either to continue the process of assimilation or to reverse it. On top of that, they faced another decision: in a new, uncertain political era, whether to side with the German-speaking rulers or with the Czech nationalists, who were growing stronger day by day and who (in the eyes of many) obviously represented the wave of the future.

Hermann Kafka's elder sister Anna married Jakob Adler, the manager of a match factory in Schüttenhofen (in southern Bohemia near Wossek and Strakonitz). Adler, reputedly a wealthy man in later life, had lived in Wossek only a few houses from where Anna was born. Before she became his wife in 1879 he had been married to Julie Toch, who died in 1872, having borne him four children. Since he was thirty-two years older than his new bride, one can perhaps assume that theirs was a marriage of convenience more typical of those days. From the records of the inhabitants of Prague – they lived in that city from 1893 to 1897 – it is clear both took pains to hide the great age difference between them. Shortly before Jakob's death in October 1897, the couple moved in with the family of Hermann Kafka's other sister, Julie Ehrmann, in Strakonitz. Franz Kafka and his sisters, Elli, Valli and Ottla, visited the childless widow there in the summer of 1905. When she died in 1936 at the age of eighty-eight, Anna was living in a Jewish nursing home in Prague.[1]

Julie (1854–1921), Hermann Kafka's younger sister, was described in somewhat uncomplimentary fashion by Kafka: 'She too has the huge face of all Father's relatives. There is something wrong and somewhat disturbing about the set or colour of her eyes.' (*D* 154) Above all she loved to talk with her brother about one of his favourite topics: the hard times of their childhood in Wossek. 'In a skimpy wet skirt, in the severe cold, she had to run out for something, the skin of her legs cracked, the skimpy skirt froze and it was only that evening, in bed, that it dried' (*D* 155).

Julie married the merchant Siegmund Ehrmann (1854–1939), by whom she had seven children. First the eldest daughter, Martha, worked in Hermann Kafka's shop on the Altstädter Ring, and later a younger daughter lived with the Kafkas for a while – all this between 1900 and 1914. The fifth child, Ida Bergmann, was able in 1957 to supply Klaus Wagenbach with many details about this branch of the family. In February 1921 Kafka wrote to his sister Ottla about this aunt: 'She cuts a curious figure in my memory; it seems to me that I never spoke a word to her, which is probably not true, but she is not without significance for me.' In this letter he also enquires about his aunt's health, showing some concern for a person whom he had previously placed in his father's camp. He probably knew of her serious illness, and his family – to avoid upsetting him in view of his own grave illness – had kept the news of her death from him.[2] Perhaps she is the aunt, mentioned in a letter to Max Brod at the beginning of May 1920, who also had a large face, an 'extraordinary listener's face: open mouth, smile, wide eyes, continual nods, and inimitable way of stretching her neck which is not only humble but seems to want to facilitate the discharge of words from the other's lips, and does so' (*L* 236–7). Listening patiently to others' stories (without any particular inner involvement) was the only sociable trait he was willing to give himself credit for.

In the 'Letter to His Father', the author characterizes his three uncles, Filip, Ludwig and Heinrich, as merrier, livelier, more spontaneous, more easy-going and less severe than Hermann Kafka (*W* 160). He must have had fewer personal memories of Heinrich, since that uncle had died in 1886 after a long illness. That he includes him in this list suggests that he had heard about him from older family members, and, as we have seen, his photograph as a young soldier served as the model for one described in *Amerika*. Heinrich, born in 1850, was a tall, handsome man. He founded the Nuremberg Fancy and Small Goods shop in Leitmeritz. Three sons, Viktor, Emil and Rudolf (1883–1942) – two of whom have already been mentioned – were borne by his wife Karoline Fleischner (1856–1929) from Kolin. After the death of her husband, Karoline continued to run his shop and married Sigmund Kohn, the manager of the business, by whom she had two sons, Fritz and Robert.

The premises of this step-uncle's firm were familiar to Kafka from his visits there in his childhood. On 9 December 1912, when he was supposed to represent his employer, the Workers' Accident Insurance Institute, at a court case in Leitmeritz, which unbeknownst to him had suddenly been postponed, Kafka found himself with several free hours and took the opportunity to visit his relatives' shop. The following day he wrote to Felice Bauer describing his aunt, to whom he was devoted: 'now an ailing but still very lively, small, round, noisy, hand-rubbing, but to me always agreeable person' (*LF* 97). Another source confirms that Aunt

The Leitmeritz relatives, *c.*1910; Rudolf (Heinrich Kafka's son), unknown, Robert Kohn, Karoline Kohn, Fritz Kohn, Sigmund Kohn

Karoline was indeed very energetic and physically very strong. Whether all who knew her found her as pleasant as Kafka remains doubtful. Among her own family she was feared, by Rudolf Kafka's wife at least. Having borne five sons herself, Karoline demanded a male heir of her daughter-in-law.[3]

Sigmund Kohn and his wife stayed much closer to Judaism than their Prague and Kolin relatives. (Emil, Karoline's son, who grew up in the Kohn family, was Kafka's only American cousin not to repudiate his Jewish origins when he emigrated to the New World.) Sigmund, especially, took his religion seriously. To marry a non-Jewish girl, a *shiksa,* for example, would have contravened all his religious principles, and he broke off all relations with his brother when the latter married a Christian girl.[4] His more assimilated relatives by marriage regarded him as the 'ghetto Jew', a man who in their view was too narrowly focused on his business and his belief (without really being orthodox). This seems to have bothered Kafka less. At any rate, his admiration remained unaffected. During the last year of his life, when he was ill and weak, the author's parents apparently wanted to enlist Karoline Kohn's assistance in finding their son an apartment in the Bohemian town of Skalitz. But she did nothing to help. 'All one learns', Kafka wrote on reading the letter she had sent them, 'is that she had worries and little time to occupy herself with such remote and questionable matters as my move.'[5] Even here he appears anxious to exonerate her.

Filip Kafka (1847–1914), Hermann's eldest brother, settled in Kolin, where he married a widow, Klara Poláček (née Hammerschlag, 1847–1908). Between 1879 and 1893 the couple had seven children: Otto, Robert, Erich, Oskar, Zdeněk, Irena and Franz, several of whom have already been introduced. It remains unclear whether Filip inherited the shop of Klara Poláček's former husband or whether he founded his own later (with his wife's financial participation). From the Registry of the Free and Manual Trades of

The Kolin relatives, before 1914; back row: Dr Josef Poláček, Zdeněk Kafka, Dr Robert Kafka, Hugo Poláček; front row: unknown, Irene (Kafka) Beck, Erich Kafka (?), Filip Kafka

the City of Kolin, one learns merely that he acquired a licence to sell straw hats in 1881, was registered subsequently as a shopkeeper and fancy-goods merchant in 1889, and was given permission to sell jewellery and linen goods in 1890. He also traded in string and rope products in Prague. The business was transferred to his son Erich (1882–1942) in 1907, but was probably dissolved after Filip's death or at the end of the First World War, since Erich later became manager of the liqueur factory of wealthier relatives in Příbram.[6]

It was Filip who apparently most lived up to Kafka's description of his three merry and easy-going uncles. According to Ida Bergmann, he was 'very affable [*gemütlich*], always jovial, always wore patent-leather shoes and a white flower in his buttonhole, liked to tell jokes that were sometimes a bit off-colour'.[7] Unlike Hermann Kafka, he lived 'in the best of harmony with his children'. But the relaxed, happy atmosphere at home could not prevent a family tragedy. His son Oskar (born 1884) entered an infantry cadet academy around 1899. (As has been said before, Kafka began a novel in his youth about two brothers, one of whom runs away to America while the other is held in a European prison. The prison may well have been inspired by his cousin's military experience.) In September 1901 Oskar made plans to change over to the Cavalry Cadet Academy in the Moravian town of Mährisch-Weisskirchen. When he did not pass the entrance exams and his career as a cavalry officer seemed doomed, he shot himself in an apartment in the city, a victim of the ambition and career pressure of the times. (Kafka too almost succumbed to those pressure, as will be seen.) 'The suicide statistics of Weisskirchen show a surprisingly high number of such cases,' the daily *Ostrauer Tagblatt* noted laconically.[8]

Another more amusing incident involving Aunt Klara Poláček proves that Kafka's memory was always well-stocked with relatives, ready to be called upon when needed. In August 1920 Milena with whom the writer had started an affair, wanting to stage a meeting with Kafka in the city of Gmünd on the border of Austria and Czechoslovakia, came up with the not very original idea of sending

Holiday photograph taken on Norderney, one of the East Frisian islands, *c.*1900; left to right: Ludwig Kafka and his wife, Filip and Klara Kafka and Franz Kafka's father

him a telegram from a fictitious Aunt Klara, whose serious illness could serve as an excuse to absent himself from his job. With melancholic irony he chides her for her lack of understanding of human nature; he would not, he claims, be able to tell this story to his superior without breaking into laughter. 'Of course, and in this you show some knowledge of human nature,' he concedes to his Czech Christian girlfriend, 'among Jews everyone has an Aunt Klara, but mine died long ago' (*LM* 139).

On the question of Judaism, the family of Filip and Klara Kafka was divided. Franz's American cousins Otto, Frank and Zdeněk (who emigrated in 1920) renounced the belief of their forefathers, which even their father Filip (like his brother Hermann) must have neglected. Of Klara Poláček's two sons from her marriage, Hugo and Josef, the latter remained a practising Jew all his life. Born in 1874, he attended high school in Kolin and later obtained a doctorate in law from the University of Prague. After his studies he opened a law office in the city of Teplitz about seventy kilometres north–north–east of Prague. Teplitz had always had a large and thriving Jewish community and around 1907 a considerable numbers of Eastern Jews settled there.[9] Although his law practice brought in a good income, the lawyer never became rich, since he spared neither time nor money to help fellow Jews in need. In the words of his daughter, he could never bring himself to refuse even one *shnorrer* (a sponge or parasite).[10]

In November 1911 Franz Kafka had occasion to remember the generous Dr Poláček. During the autumn Kafka had attended the performances of an eastern Jewish actors' troupe at Prague's Café Savoy. Impressed and at times even deeply moved by their naïve vitality, so different from the assimilatory bias of his own upbringing, the writer tried not merely to absorb all he could of the new atmosphere from a distance, but to get close to the actors and to help them in small ways. When they prepared to leave Prague for Nuremberg, he advised them to stop off in some smaller town before pressing on to their final destination. Someone in the group mentioned Teplitz as a possible stopping place and Kafka supported the idea enthusiastically – as he notes in his diary – because he could then give them a letter of recommendation to 'Dr P.' (*D* 111). He was obviously well aware of his relative's readiness to aid Jews. A member of the Teplitz Lodge of B'nai Brith, later a member of the executive of the Jewish Community Council and the Cultural Advisory Council as well as Director of the Jewish Hospital, Dr Poláček was in a good position to make the actors' stay in Teplitz agreeable.

In his numerous autobiographical fragments, Kafka attempts to define, explain and even justify himself and his peculiar development by contrasting himself with others. Comparisons with relatives offered excellent scope. Thus in the 'Letter to His Father' he maintains that even without the influence of his father he would still have 'become a weakly, timid, hesitant, restless person, neither [a] Robert Kafka nor [a] Karl Hermann' (*W* 159). Karl Hermann, of whom more will be said shortly, presented the type of the urbane man, well versed in business dealings. Kafka was affected much more deeply and enduringly by his cousin Robert (1881–1922), whose seduction he incorporated into *Amerika*. Max Brod reports that on his sickbed not long before his death Kafka remembered the vitality of his cousin when at the *Schwimmschule,* a public swimming establishment on the

Studio portrait of the newly-weds Dr Robert Kafka and Elsa Robiček, *c*.1914

Moldau river in Prague, the young man 'jumped into the water and rolled around in it with the power of a beautiful, wild animal, his body glistening, his eyes shining brightly'.[11]

After obtaining his law doctorate, Robert opened an office in Kolin and later moved it to Prague. He was, as Kafka himself noted, 'very busy, with work as well as with pleasure'. Many leading men and women from Czech intellectual and political life regularly visited his house. His wife, Elsa Robiček, was related to the eminent Prague physician Dr Egmont Münzer, with whose help Kafka later tried to get his young friend Robert Klopstock admitted to medical school in Prague (*L* 298, 306, 313, 315, 318).[12] On the occasion of Robert's wedding in July 1916 Kafka bought a wedding present for the young couple on his parents' behalf. His tastes were obviously considerably closer to Robert's than his father's. He chose a picture by the Czech painter Willi Nowak, whose purchase he entrusted to Max Brod (*L* 116–17, 119). Robert's political views also came much closer to the author's. In contrast to his other brothers, notably Otto, who seems to have had leanings

Prague at the turn of the century.
Top left to right: coffee vendor; the fruit

Above: hot chestnut seller; below: a
Bierhaus

nade on the Franzensquai; below: the Graben, the main street in Prague

towards Germany, Robert Kafka stood firmly in the Czech nationalist camp as a member of the Young Czech movement, and even during the First World War he did not hide his active espousal of the cause of Czech independence. After Franz Kafka's death, Max Brod claims to have learned that both he and Robert had taken part in meetings of the political 'Klub mladých' (Club of the Young Ones).[13]

Ludwig Kafka (1857–1911), Hermann Kafka's youngest brother, followed him to Prague in the 1880s. On 3 January 1886 he announced in the *Prager Tagblatt* that he had bought the existing fancy-goods shop 'Hermann Kafka' at 651 Stephansgasse and that he planned to keep it on, offering 'a greatly increased stock'.[14] He pointed to his 'lengthy experience in this line of business as well as his comfortable means', which would enable him 'to serve the valued customer in the best and least expensive manner'. Exactly how long he was able to carry out his intention is not known. According to Ida Bergmann, he was honest and upright but not suited to business and could only with great difficulty support himself, his wife Laura and his two daughters. Records show that the family moved to Teplitz in November 1905, so it can be assumed that his shop had gone under before that date.[15] Some time before his early death in 1911 he returned to Prague to become a bookkeeper for the insurance company Germania.

Both Ludwig's daughters worked in an office. (It is not clear if by 'office' Ida Bergmann meant Hermann Kafka's shop.) Hedwig, born in 1887, married Karl Löw, a man from Karlsbad. She is probably the cousin Kafka describes in his letter to Felice Bauer of 5 October 1916, who with her husband and two-year-old child had come to visit the Kafka family that day. (The child would have been Lilly Löw, born in December 1913.)[16] Jokingly he said that his description of the bourgeois family represented his contribution to a 'Chamber of Horrors' which could be added to an exhibition, 'Mother and Infant', which Felice had visited in Berlin. Kafka was much closer to Ludwig's younger daughter Irma. Born in 1889, she was given a job in Hermann Kafka's shop after the death of her father, probably some time during the war. She and the author's

Franz Kafka's sister, Ottla, (left)
and cousin Irma in Zürau, 1917/18

youngest and favourite sister Ottla became very close
friends, until Ottla decided in April 1917 to flee her father's
repressive household and accept work on the farm owned
by the family of her brother-in-law Karl Hermann in Zürau.

Franz must have seen Irma often in his father's shop in the
Kinsky Palace on the Altstädter Ring; she was the first
person he confided in about his lung haemorrhage, the
harbinger of the tuberculosis that was to kill him (O 40). The
author characterizes her in the 'Letter to His Father' as effic-
ient, intelligent, hard-working, modest, trustworthy, unsel-
fish, loyal (W 188). For Kafka, she epitomized the devastating
impact of Hermann Kafka's educational endeavours:

The fact was that, under pressure from us too of course, she came near to
being in the relation, to you, of one of your own children, and the power
of your personality to bend others was, even in her case, so great that
what developed in her (admittedly only in relation to you and, it is to be
hoped, without the deeper suffering a child experiences) was forgetful-
ness, carelessness, a grim sardonic sort of humour, and perhaps even a
shade of defiance, in so far as she was capable of that at all, and in all this I
am not taking any account whatsoever of the fact that she was inclined to
be ailing, and not very happy in other respects either, and that she was
burdened by the bleakness of her life at home. What was so illuminating
to me in your relation to her, you yourself summed up in a remark that
became classical for us, one that was almost blasphemous, but at the same
time extraordinary evidence of the *naïvety* of your way of treating people:
'The late lamented in the Lord has left me a damned mess [*Schweinestall*:
literally, 'pigsty'] to clear up.' (W 188–9)

Hermann Kafka's outburst about her leaving him with such a mess was most likely uttered shortly after Irma left his employ (in 1918?), in order to prepare for her imminent marriage to Gustave Vesecky. To appreciate the full force of Kafka's account as well as of his father's curse, one should bear in mind that when he wrote this famous letter to his father in November 1919 Irma had been dead for scarcely six months. She had died on 29 May 1919 after a sudden, violent illness (probably Spanish influenza).[17] Under the circumstances, this reminder of his tyrannical behaviour and of his uncouth outburst was below the belt, for even someone as thick-skinned as Hermann Kafka must have been ashamed of the sharp contrast between his perceived treatment of Irma and his professed sense of family. True, Kafka, aware of its emotional charge, never sent the letter.

On Kafka's mother's side of the family there were, besides the two brothers Alfred and Joseph, who lived abroad, Richard Löwy and the half-brothers Rudolf and Siegfried. The latter, born in 1867, was the only fully fledged academic of the family. He completed his secondary education and medical training in Prague. During his years at the medical school, from 1887 on, he was a member of the Lese- und Redehalle deutscher Studenten in Prag, a well-known students' intellectual society at the university which Kafka later joined.[18] He eventually set up in practice as a country doctor in the little town of Triesch on the border between Bohemia and Moravia. Kafka seems to have regarded him as his favourite uncle; he spent part of his summer vacation with him when he was a student, and it was Siegfried who gave him medical advice during his last, long illness. The age difference between the two was not all that great. Siegfried might have seemed more like an elder brother to Kafka, who started his studies about nine years after Löwy ended his.

Richard Löwy (1857–1938) became a merchant and owned a workers' clothing shop, later (1919) a small business making under garments, on the Ovocný trh (Fruit Market) in Prague's Old City, not far from Hermann Kafka's business. He married Hedwig Trebitsch (1870–1922), by whom he had four children, Martha (born 1891),

Family photograph, *c.*1908; sitting: Kafka's mother and father, Aunt Julie from Strakonitz; behind: Uncle Siegfried and Uncle Richard and his wife Hedwig

Max (1893–1944), Franz (1896–1942) and Gertrud (1900–42).[19] Franz Kafka characterized him as a man very different from his own father, a married man who had not 'collapsed' under the weight of marriage and who could have served as an example of how to overcome his fear of binding himself for life (*W* 214). Richard seems to have possessed some standing in the community; after his wife's death he gave money for the creation of a small park in Prague which was to bear his wife's name, the Hedwig-Löwy-Trebitsch Gardens.[20] Cousin Martha was renowned in family circles for her beauty; her brother Max seems to have had Zionist sympathies and is probably the Max Löwy who ran as a candidate for the Jewish Social Democratic Workers' Party in the parliamentary elections of October 1929. During the Nazi occupation Max Löwy held the position of Treasurer (*Finanzverwalter*) of the Jewish community in Prague. In December 1942, shortly after seeing to the burial of his uncle Siegfried, who had been hounded to death by the Nazis, he

Above left and right: Rudolf Löwy and his half-brothers Richard and Siegfried (below), the country doctor

was himself deported to the Theresienstadt ghetto and from there in 1944 to the gas chambers of Auschwitz.[21]

For Kafka, possibly the most significant of the uncles who stayed at home was Rudolf Löwy (1861–1921), a 'shy, excessively modest' man, like himself 'quiet (I less so)', who worked as a bookkeeper in a brewery in the Prague suburb of Košiř and was 'condemned' to live with and look after his father Jakob, whom he did not get on with (*D* 403). He converted to Catholicism and remained a well-preserved bachelor to the end of his life. From an account that Kafka read and from stories he had heard of him in his childhood, he knew how much Rudolf (like himself) had 'had to contend (inwardly) with women' (*D* 403). To Hermann Kafka he was a ludicrous figure, the 'family fool', though Franz himself later developed in his father's eyes into 'the fool of the new generation of the family, the fool somewhat altered to meet the needs of a different period' (*D* 143, *L* 309).

RICHARD LÖWY

VÝRÓBA PRÁDLA	WÄSCHE-ERZEUGUNG
PRAHA,	**PRAG,**
Ovocný trh č. 10 I. posch.	Obstmarkt Nr. 10 I. Stock.
Čís. poštovní spoř. 10.038.	Postspark.-Konto 10.038.

TELEFON 45-VIII.

Hermann family wedding *c*.1914; standing left to right: unknown, Karl and Elli Hermann (Franz's sister), Rudolf Hermann, Paul Hermann, Ida Hermann, Walter Braun, Hugo Hermann, Liesl Braun, Ernst Hermann; sitting left to right: unknown, Herrmann and Julie Kafka (Franz's parents) with their grandson, Felix Hermann (Elli's son), Leopold Hermann, Wilma Trauer (née Hermann), Max Trauer, Sofie Hermann, Mr Trauer senior, Mathilde Braun, Dr Alfred Braun

8

Lawyers and Factory Owners: The Richer and More Successful Kafkas

When contemplating Hermann Kafka's career and social ascent, one must remember that his remarkable accomplishments were overshadowed by the successes of other members of the *mishpocheh,* especially those of his two elder cousins Angelus and Friedrich, who along with six other brothers and sisters were born and grew up in the village of Wossek, house number 30. In 1866 after he had been in business for several years and after contemplating a commercial apprenticeship, Angelus (born 1837) founded a vinegar and liqueur factory in Strakonitz. When he started a second one in 1872 he moved the seat of his operations to Prague.[1] For more than forty years his firm's office was at 13 Plattnergasse in the Old City, the former Jewish quarter, a stone's throw from Hermann Kafka's business. Large advertisements for his wares, notably the fruit liqueur Morella or a digestif called Amarentino, appeared regularly in the *Prager Tagblatt.* Thanks to his enormous diligence he increased his business considerably in both variety and volume. As the *Tagblatt* reported in an obituary published in August 1908, he owned besides a house and other property in Prague a large vineyard in the town of Podhoř near the city, and he had developed his wholesale wine business 'into one of the biggest enterprises in this line not only in Bohemia but in all of Austria'.[2]

For a long time Angelus was regarded as the patriarch of the Kafka *mishpocheh.* Between 1875 and 1880 he gathered other family members around him. For a number of years he cared for his father Samuel in his house in the Plattnergasse and provided lodging for an uncle, Salamon Kafka (born in 1819).[3] Another of Angelus Kafka's uncles, Leopold (1829–1902), a cab driver, was living at the same address in 1875. Three years later he moved up in the world by becoming the proprietor of the tavern U bílího lva (At the sign of White Lion), also in the Plattnergasse and probably connected with the liqueur and wine firm of his nephew. There followed a number of cafés under his management, among them a Café Kafka (around 1888), exact address unknown, the Grand Café London (*c.* 1891–3), entrance in Zeltnergasse and the Fruit Market, the Café Salon (1897) at 549 Altstädter Ring.[4] Perhaps the most persuasive testimony to Angelus Kafka's status in the family is the fact that Hermann Kafka chose him to be Franz's godfather in 1883.[5]

Angelus' younger brothers equalled if they did not surpass him in business acumen and success. Friedrich (1849–1908) briefly entered his brother's firm as a partner, then started his own liqueur factory in the southern Bohemian city of Příbram in 1877, adding a branch in Klosterneuburg near Vienna (which was run for many years by his son Hugo). His appointment as purveyor to the imperial and royal household indicates that he was as well known in the Empire as Angelus. A third brother, Heinrich (1855–1917), also made a name for himself by opening a liqueur-manufacturing firm in Prague.[6]

This branch of the Kafka family also gained a solid reputation in the field of law. Dr Moritz Kafka (1844–1924), another of Angelus' brothers, attended school in Prague, then studied law there and in the Austrian city of Graz. After obtaining a law doctorate from Graz he set up his own practice in Prague in 1879. According to the German newspaper *Bohemia,* he was considered 'one of the best-known and respected Prague lawyers and one of the most valued members of the German community in Prague'.[7] He was also held in high esteem as a sharp-witted jurist and an

Dr Moritz Kafka (left) and Dr Bruno Kafka

'enthusiastic promoter' of German clubs and organizations in his native city. His wife Martha came from the distinguished and wealthy Prague Jewish families of Bondy and Tedesco. For many years he sat on the disciplinary council of the Chamber of Barristers and also acted as that body's legal representative. And when Hermann Kafka started up in business in 1882–3, he chose his cousin Moritz to complete the necessary fomalities at the commercial court.[8]

Only Moritz's son Bruno (1881–1931) could outshine his father's achievements. He too studied law at the German university in Prague and became an *Assistent* to the then famous Professor of Jurisprudence Horaz Krasnopolski. After receiving his doctorate in law in 1904 Bruno continued his studies in Leipzig and Heidelberg, and was formally inducted as university lecturer in his native city in 1907, at a time when Franz Kafka's future in the field of law seemed very uncertain. In 1912 Bruno was granted the title of associate professor, and further titles and honours followed: full professor, dean, member of the academic senate of the German university in Prague, and finally rector of that institution. He too made a good marriage: his wife Hanna was the daughter of Maximilian Bondy-Bondrop, engineer and director of the firm Moritz Bondy.[9] In an obituary after Bruno's untimely death in 1931, the law journal *Prager juristische Zeitschrift* wrote, 'Thus his life from beginning to end was entwined with the city of Prague and as a true German son of this city he always represented the interests of German society here, with all his energy and with all the political talent at his disposal.'[10] Bruno's political talent flowered during the First World War, when he assumed the leadership of the Progressive Party and also became director of the War Welfare Office in Prague. After the war he continued his political activity in the new Czechoslovak Republic as member of parliament for the German Democratic Freedom Party. Franz Kafka greatly admired this energetic and successful relative, although he had reservations about his German nationalist tendencies, which had surfaced during their time together at university.

Kafka knew Bruno from his days in the Lese- und Redehalle, the intellectual student fraternity of which his uncle Siegfried had been a member. Kafka joined in 1901, when Bruno, like his father Moritz, had already established himself not only as an active and enthusiastic member but as a leader in almost every endeavour the organization engaged in. In every year of his membership (1899–1903) Bruno occupied one post or other in the Redehalle, usually high executive positions. He led the drive to raise money for the construction of a new building for the society. (Kafka only made it to the post of secretary in the Literature and Art section in the summer term of 1904.) During his student days Bruno also gave many talks in the Redehalle, mainly in the Law section, but also at least once in the Literature section on the (today quite unknown) nineteenth-century realist author Max Dreyer, under the title 'Max Dreyer's Novel *Hans* and Its Special Place in Realist Literature'.[11] An interest in the arts was then fashionable among students; it showed that one was well bred and versatile. It was not meant to go much further than that. Thus Franz Kafka could note that his parents fully expected his devotion to literature to subside into the casual interest of the educated man.

Against the backdrop of the successes of the *mishpocheh*, one must now consider Franz Kafka's career. Having completed his law studies in lacklustre fashion, he had come to recognize during his one year of articles in the chambers of Dr Richard Löwy that in view of his limited interest in the law he would never build up a legal practice of his own. His positions first with the Assicurazioni Generali and from 1908 with the Workers' Accident Insurance Institute offered few possibilities for advancement. (Only gradually did his employers at the semi-governmental insurance company come to appreciate his qualities). It is doubtful whether his achievements satisfied the expectations of his father. Even after his son's death Hermann seems to have called him 'poor Franz', referring to his lack of material wealth.[12]

Late in the summer of 1911 the decision was reached in the Kafka family to found the Prager Asbestwerke Hermann & Co.[13] The two registered partners were to be Franz Kafka and his brother-in-law Karl Hermann. The recently published critical edition of Kafka's diaries contains the draft of a letter, hitherto unknown, from Kafka to Karl's younger brother Paul (who later joined the firm) which confirms the long-held suspicion that Kafka himself was one of the prime movers in the undertaking. He had, he writes, advised his father to loan Karl Hermann money to invest in the firm, had convinced his Uncle Alfred to contribute and had himself put some money into the venture. Apparently Karl's father Leopold Hermann contributed a large sum.[14]

Karl Hermann was a sharp, self-assured businessman with a touch of the debonair man of the world.[15] (He was the first in the Kafka family to acquire a gramophone and played records on it when learning to dance the tango.) Hermann Kafka admired and distrusted him at one and the same time. So son Franz was to learn some business sense from him while representing his father's interests, 'supervising him' as he himself put it. (*L* 89).

In October and November 1911 meetings took place between Karl Hermann, Franz Kafka and the lawyer Dr Robert Kafka to draw up the partnership contract. Robert Kafka was not the cousin from Kolin but the son of the liqueur and wine manufacturer Heinrich. In his diary Kafka gives a detailed sketch of this man, a loquacious individual totally immersed in questions of court jurisdiction, reminiscent of the lawyer Huld in *The Trial* (*D* 75). Another diary entry describing one of the preparatory meetings reveals the wider implications of the founding of the factory:

This page: Robert Kafka; next page: application to the commercial court of Prague for the inclusion of the Prager Asbestwerke Hermann & Co. on the business register, January 1912.

When the lawyer, in reading the agreement to me, came to a passage concerning my possible future wife and possible children, I saw across from me a table with two large chairs and a smaller one around it. At the thought that I should never be in a position to seat in these or any other three chairs myself, my wife, and my child, there came over me a yearning for this happiness so despairing from the very start that in my excitement I asked the lawyer the only question I had left after the long reading, which at once revealed my complete misunderstanding of a rather long section of the agreement that had just been read. (*D* 110)

Kafka shows clearly how the founding of a business and a family are entwined. Not only was a small industrial empire being planned here, but also its continuation in future generations. Subtly and with humour Kafka suggests with this incident that the two spheres are alien to one another and that he cannot partake of either.

His part in urging the establishment of the factory in 1911 weighed heavily on Kafka's conscience in the following years. 'I bear the chief blame for the establishment of the factory,' he wrotes only a year later to Max Brod, and almost half-heartedly added in mitigation, 'though I must have assumed this blame in a dream' (*L* 89). His father's comment, recorded by Kafka in his diary in 1914, was coarser but more vivid, and leaves no doubt that he held Franz responsible: 'You talked [literally: danced] me into it' (*D* 322). A few years later in the 'Letter to His Father' Kafka paraphrased a similar reproach: the son had left the factory on his father's hands and left him 'in the lurch' (*W* 158).

K.K. HANDELSGERICHT in PRAG
EINGELANGT 13. JANUAR 1912
FACH 6 BEILAGEN

507
V 254

1

An das

k.k. H a n d e l s g e r i c h t

in P r a g !

Karl Hermann, Kaufmann in Prag, Mariengasse 18 n.

und Dr. Franz Kafka, Beamte in Prag V. Niklasstrasse 36

vertreten durch

Dr. Robert Kafka, Advokaten in Prag

melden die Errichtung einer offenen
Handelsgesellschaft unter der Firma:
"Pražská továrna na osinkové zboži,
Hermann & spol." oder deutsch: "Prager
Asbestwerke Hermann & Co." zur Ein-
tragung in das Handelsregister.

E i n f a c h.

1 Rubrik, Beilage A - E orig.

Right: drawing of the facade of the Prager Asbestwerke on Bořijova Street in the Žižkov district of Prague. This building appears on the plan below as number 918; the factory is behind it beyond the courtyard

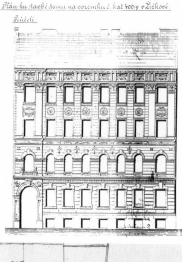

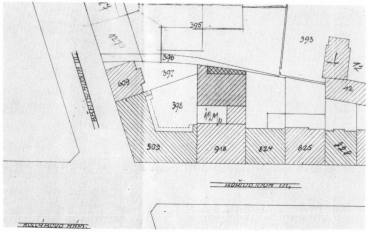

Whether Kafka agreed to participate because at one time he felt he could do the necessary work without disturbing his routine or whether he agreed because he wanted to placate his father with this gesture, one thing is certain: he soon learned to hate both the factory and his role as factory-owner. In December 1911 he began to hear the first reproaches from his father for neglecting his duties (*D* 137); shortly afterwards he uttered his first complaint in the diary, almost a scream of pain: 'The torment that the factory causes me' (*D* 155).

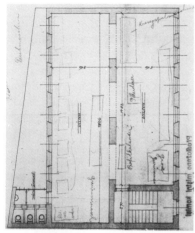

Below: the low building in the foreground is the former Asbestwerke factory; the plan (left), oriented in the same direction, shows the ground floor: the pencilled squares show the positioning of various industrial machines

The Yiddish word *naches* denotes the satisfaction or even gratification that parents feel at the achievements of their children (not just in the sphere of business). So every parent can expect to experience *naches* from dutiful children as they grow up and settle into a career and married life. The expectations of Kafka's parents were no different, though given the precedents set by the *mishpocheh* they might have fixed them too high. But they were confident that their son would turn out all right in the end – a confidence not shared by Kafka himself. A conversation he had with his mother in

December 1911 showed him that she naïvely believed that it was only a question of time before he straightened himself out. 'She considers me a healthy young man who suffers a little from the notion that he is ill,' Kafka wrote in his diary. 'This notion will disappear by itself with time, marriage, of course, and having children would put an end to it best of all. Then my interest in literature would also be reduced to the degree that is perhaps necessary for an educated man. A matter-of-fact, undisturbed interest in my profession or in the factory or in whatever may come to hand will appear' (*D* 143). Once again marriage and the founding of family are seen as closely related to a useful activity such as running the factory, all in the hope that the son will get back on the right track. When in August 1912 Kafka met Felice Bauer, to whom he was immediately attracted, it must have appeared to him that now his mother's wish could be fulfilled.

In 1912 new duties weighed more and more heavily on the would-be industrialist. His parents' desire to see him as a well-to-do bourgeois accumulating ever greater riches collided head on with his determination to spend his time writing. Their desire was also at odds with his ideological sympathies, which lay on the side of his workers. According to official documents there were twenty-five workers in the factory at 918 Žižkov (an annexe to the apartment block into which Karl Hermann's father moved in 1914). They worked at fourteen machines driven by a 14 h.p. petrol engine and produced asbestos and rubber goods of all kinds, high-pressure plates, and insulation and packaging materials.[16] 'They are at the mercy of the pettiest power,' Kafka wrote of the girls working in the factory, 'and haven't enough calm understanding to recognize this power and placate it by a glance, a bow' (*D* 179). One should also note – what was undiscovered until now – that at this time Kafka the insurance agency employee was involved in the creation of an Association of Officials of the Workers' Accident Insurance Institute, the closest these white-collar workers could come to forming a union; Kafka was treasurer of the Association for a brief period.[17] Thus Kafka occupied the two conflicting positions of factory-owner and union leader at the same time. Above all, though, Kafka saw his writing endangered by his new part-time occupation. His work schedule at the Workers' Accident Insurance Institute, 'simple cycle' (*einfache Frequenz*), called for his presence in the office until half-past one or two in the afternoon (without a break at noon). His afternoons, normally spent gathering strength for his late-night writing sessions, were now often taken up with work for the Asbestwerke. Time and energy were in short supply. There were unpleasant family rows about the firm which only compounded his feelings of guilt. The money set aside for the inital months of the venture proved to be insufficient and Karl Hermann had to ask for more from his father-in-law. Kafka composed a 'good letter to Uncle Alfred about the factory' (*D* 202) – to ask for money and perhaps advice – and otherwise dutifully accepted blame from father, mother, brother-in-law and anyone else who proffered it. Even his favourite sister Ottla failed to stand by him (*L* 89). 'And I with my scribblings,' he exclaimed in exasperation at the end of a diary entry describing one evening's particualrly acrimonious debate (*D* 202). The family's misfortune affected him to such a degree that he was ready to disparage, if only temporarily, the very activity to which he felt himself most suited.

During the night of 22/23 September 1912, the factory episodes merged with his meeting with Felice to form the foundation of his story 'The Judgement'. The young businessman Georg Bendemann, whose situation is presented to the reader soon after the opening lines of the story, has become engaged to Frieda Brandenfeld, and successfully expanded his father's business. His friend's firm in Russia, however, is going downhill, and a direct comparison is made: 'The figures quoted were microscopic by comparison with the range of Georg's present operations' (*IPS* 47). Moreover, Georg's engagement means that he will soon start his own family, bringing him success on the two fronts where Kafka could not join battle. Georg's victories are, of course, at the expense of his father, who has gone into physical and mental decline.

The friend in Russia, a failure, a confirmed bachelor, corresponds more closely to Kafka's own reality, whereas Georg is the true sense of the word a fictional character

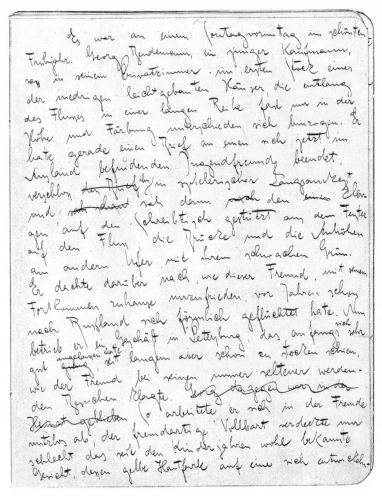

First page of the autograph manuscript of 'The Judgement' written in a diary on the night of 22/3 September, 1912

trying to gain substance. He attempts to remind his father of his friend in St Petersburg so that he can compare himself favourably with him. If his father can be tricked into accepting the friend as a separate entity, a far-off failure, then Georg has created an existence for himself. But the father refuses to be duped; he refuses to let the friend vegetate as his son's opposite in a strange land. He conjures him up as the true son: 'Of course I know your friend. He would have been a son after my own heart' (*IPS* 55). To emphasize that the friend represents the more real person, Kafka follows up the father's outburst with the words, 'His friend in St. Petersburg, whom his father suddenly knew so well, touched his [Georg's] imagination as never before' (*IPS* 55). When the father rises up with renewed vigour to sentence his son to death, he is merely sweeping a fictional, papier-mâché figure off the table. Thus Kafka is able to satisfy both himself and his own father; he writes what he later describes as a perfect story and lets his father, acting as a character in the story, expose and destroy his fiction. The charge by Georg's father that his son is both 'an innocent child' and 'a devilish human being' (*IPS* 58) can be explained by Kafka's having intentionally blurred the line between fact and fiction. As a fictional creation of the author, Georg is indeed innocent; he cannot help being what he is (successful in business and marriage). As an extension of the real son's (Kafka's) being, a character who wishes to make use of the fiction of the son no parent could reject, he is a devil. This represents an even more radical mingling of autobiography and fiction than the instances in *Amerika* where Kafka seems to be commenting through Karl on his source material.

The destruction of a fictional protagonist similar to Georg Bendemann is carried out in the story 'The Metamorphosis', begun in the middle of November 1912. Gregor Samsa is not an independent businessman like Bendemann; he is a travelling salesman. Constantly under pressure to make sales, constantly held in suspicion by a distrustful boss, he toils to earn money to maintain himself and his family in a middle-class existence. What is more, he has to pay off the business debts of his bankrupt parents. But this life of great sacrifice for his mother, father and sister is actually over before the story begins and is recapitulated only in Gregor's memory. Kafka cleverly opens his story with the protagonist's transformation, since which he has become a burden on his family rather than its saviour. The life of sacrifice is the sentimental fiction Gregor might like to remember; the story of his insect life, which actually comprises the body of the text, is the long-savoured

Above left: Felice Bauer and her mother, *c.*1911; right: Julie Wohryzek during the First World War; next page: drawing by Franz Kafka

punishment for dreams of such saccharine and indeed impossible dutifulness.

In October 1912 the crisis at the Prager Asbestwerke reached its climax for Kafka. It came to the point where he even thought of jumping out of a window, and Brod took the threat of suicide seriously enough to write to the author's mother.[18] As a result Karl Hermann's younger brother Paul, 'a fool in all matters except business, and even in business matters to a considerable extent' (*L* 88), took over Kafka's duties and was eventually made a partner in 1914. Until its dissolution in 1917, the Asbestwerke repeatedly surfaced in Kafka's life, especially in his relationship with Felice Bauer. The first somewhat embarrassed mention of his participation in the venture is contained in the letter of 1 November 1912 (*LF* 22). It appears as a half-hearted attempt to impress the independent young girl from Berlin with the suggestion that he too has a practical side. For Felice the factory simply meant security. If Kafka wanted to marry her, their life together should rest on the best possible financial foundation, at least one that would allow them a solid middle-class existence. 'Why do you have more understanding for the factory than for me,' he remonstrated with her (*LF* 444). He demanded 'a fantastic life arranged in the interest of my work'; she, 'indifferent to every mute request', wanted 'the average: a comfortable home, an interest on my part in the factory' (*D* 328). Clearly he recognized that she was actually in his parent's camp and that after marrying him she would try to drag him over into it, whether she was aware of it now or not. Julie Kafka called the process 'remoulding', and she had hoped that Felice in her wisdom would quietly bring it about (*LF* 46). But actually it was this vision of a life given over to bourgeois values that brought about the failure of Kafka's two engagements to Felice. The only other occasion Kafka came close to marrying was in 1919 when he became engaged for a short time to Julie Wohryzek, but by then his illness and Julie's age, at which she 'hardly had anything left of her longing for children', had made a large family an unlikely prospect and the trials and tribulatons of the factory were no more than a distant, unpleasant memory. As he wrote to Julie's older sister Käthe, he was at this point not even inwardly a merchant, but merely an official, a member of the lowest class of European professionals, 'nervous, totally lost to all the dangers of literature, with weak lungs, and tiredly trying to avoid the petty paper work at the office'.[19]

Abbreviations

Passages from Kafka's works are quoted from published English translations, cited under the following abbreviations, and to which acknowledgment is made:

A   *America*, trans. Willa and Edwin Muir (London: Secker & Warburg, 1949)

D   *The Diaries of Franz Kafka 1910–1923*, ed. Max Brod, trans. Joseph Kresh (1910–1913) and Martin Greenberg with the cooperation of Hannah Arendt (1914–1923) (London: Secker & Warburg, 1949)

IPS   *In the Penal Settlement: Tales and Short Prose Works*, trans. Ernst Kaiser and Eithne Wilkins (London: Secker & Warburg, 1949) (includes 'The Judgement')

L   *Letters to Friends, Family, and Editors*, trans. Richard and Clara Winston (London: John Calder, 1978)

LF   *Letters to Felice*, ed. Erich Heller and Jürgen Born, trans. James Stern and Elizabeth Duckworth (London: Secker & Warburg, 1974)

LM   *Letters to Milena*, ed. Willy Haas, trans. James and Tania Stern (London: Secker & Warburg, 1953)

T   *The Trial*, Definitive Edition, trans. Willa and Edwin Muir, rev. E.M. Butler (London: Secker & Warburg, 1956)

W   *Wedding Preparations in the Country and other posthumous prose writings*, trans. Ernst Kaiser and Eithne Wilkins (London: Secker & Warburg, 1954) (includes 'Letter to His Father' and 'A Report to an Academy')

Notes

1 Kafka's Family Feeling

[1] See the headnote above for a list of abbreviations used in referring to Kafka's works cited or quoted in translation in the text.

[2] Leo Rosten, *The Joys of Yiddish* (New York: Pocket Books, Washington Square Press, 1970), pp. 251–2.

[3] L.B. Kreitner, 'Kafka as a Young Man', *Connecticut Review*, vol. 3, no. 2 (April 1970), 28–9. As regards the assimilated Jews' 'fear' of Yiddish, compare an incident recounted by George Clare in *Last Waltz in Vienna: The Destruction of a Family 1842–1942* (London: Pan Books, 1982), pp. 84–5, and Kafka's own talk on *Jargon*, 'Rede über die jiddische Sprache' ('An Introductory Talk on the Yiddish Language', *W* 418–22).

[4] Dominik Kostelezky, *Handbuch der Gesetze in Unterthanssachen für Kreisämter, andere politische Behörden, Grundherrschaften, obrigkeitliche Aemter, Advokaten, Justiziäre, und Unterthanen im Königreiche Böhmen* (Prague: Bei E.W. Enders, 1815), pp. 384–5. 'Jüdische Kultusgemeinde Strakonitz, Geburtsmatrik Strakonitz', November 1839–2 November 1861, entries 105, p. 40, and 132, p. 46, 105 a GII, HBMa 1936, Archivní spravá, Prague.

[5] Jaroslav Polák-Rokycana, 'Dějiny Židů v Písku', *Die Juden und Judengemeinden Böhmens in Vergangenheit und Gegenwart: Ein Sammelwerk* I, ed. Hugo Gold (Brünn-Prague: Jüdischer Buch-und Kunstverlag, 1934), pp. 489–500.

[6] *Die Notablenversammlung der Israeliten Böhmens in Prag, ihre Berathungen und Beschlüsse* (Mit statistischen Tabellen über die israelitischen Gemeinden, Synagogen Schulen und Rabbinate in Böhmen), hrsg. v. Albert Kohn (Wien, Verlag von Leopold Sommer, 1852), pp. 411–12.

[7] 'Anzeigezettel zur Zählung der Bevölkerung und der wichtigen häuslichen Nutzthiere nach dem Stande vom 31. October 1857,' Městký archiv v Podiěbradech (Okresní archiv v Nimburce).

[8] *Allgemeines Adressbuch der Königl. Hauptstadt Prag, der Vorstädte Karolinenthal, etc.* (Prague: Verlag der Bohemia, 1875), p. 105.

2 Into the Belle Époque

[1] Max Brod, *Franz Kafka. Eine Biographie* (Frankfurt am Main: S. Fischer Verlag, 1962), p. 12. The spelling of the name Loewy is the one both brothers used throughout their life. The same holds true for the name Joseph.

[2] Brod, p. 9.

[3] Data about the youth of the brothers Loewy: *Seznam Brancù 1838–1887* Městký archiv v Podiě-

bradech (Okresní archiv v Nimburce). Further information about Alfred Loewy from his application for French citizenship. ('Demande de Naturalisation') No. 4442373 in the Archives Nationales, Paris.
[4] The *Politisches-Geschäfts-Protokoll* (*Political Business Protocol*) in the Okresní archiv v Nimburce shows that Joseph applied for a passport in November 1881 and received it at the beginning of 1882. *Bulletin du Canal Interocéanique*, 2e année, numéro 36, 15 février 1881, p. 323, p. 1.
[5] Biographical material about Philippe Bunau-Varilla: Gustave Anguizola, *Philippe Bunau-Varilla: The Man Behind the Panama Canal* (Chicago: Nelson Hall, 1980); Charles D. Ameringer, 'The Panama Canal Lobby of Philippe Bunau-Varilla and William Nelson Cromwell', *American Historical Review*, vol. 68, no. 2 (January 1963), 346–63; 'Bunau-Varilla, Russia, and the Panama Canal', *Journal of Inter-American Studies and World Affairs*, vol. 12, no. 3 (July 1970), 328–38; *Dictionnaire de Biographies Françaises*, ed. M. Prévost and R. d'Amat, vol 7 (Paris: Librairie Letouzey et Ane, 1956), p. 667.
[6] The Papers of Philippe Bunau-Varilla, Manuscripts Division, Library of Congress, Washington DC, Box 1 (abbreviated: BV Papers).
[7] Letter which Loewy used to legitimize himself as the individual with power of attorney and which appears in the minutes of the Crédit Municipal Canadien, 'Registre des Déliberations', 'Séances du Conseil d'Administration', 23 September 1907, in the Archives Régionales de l'Université du

Québec à Rimouski. The text of the extract from the minutes reads: 'M. Loewy, qui a occupé des fonctions importantes à Panama, au Congo et en Chine, a acquis une grande expérience des affaires d'entreprises industrielles et de travaux publics.'
[8] Maron J. Simon, *The Panama Affair* (New York: Charles Scribner's Sons, 1971).
[9] Loewy's correspondence with P. Gautron, the Administrateur judiciaire de la Compagnie de Panama, September 1891, BV Papers, Box 1.
[10] Reprint of a letter from Philippe Bunau-Varilla, BV Papers, Box 12.
[11] Letter from Alfred Loewy to Philippe Bunau-Varilla, 26 June 1906, BV Papers, Box 12.
[12] René J. Cornet, *La Bataille du Rail*, quatrième édition revue et augmentée (Brussels: Éditions L. Cuypers, 1958), pp. 305–6.
[13] *La Libre Parole*, 3ème année, No. 791, lundi, le 22 janvier 1894, p. 2, col. 1.

3 From Matadi to Montreux

[1] *Mouvement Géographique*, no. 3, 2 August 1891, p. 4, col. 3. Information about Joseph Loewy's work in the Congo comes from his personal file deposited with Otraco, the company that followed the Compagnie du Chemin de Fer du Congo. Those files now rest with the Ministère des Finances, Administration provisoire des questions financières du Congo et du Ruanda-Urundi, Brussels.
[2] A spine-chilling description of cannibalism by Nicolas Tobbak is contained in 'Attaques et défense

de la station des Falls: 18 mai 1893', *Les Belges au Congo. Notices Biographiques*, ed. Édouard Janssens and Albert Cateaux, vol. II (Antwerp: J. Van Hille-De Backer, 1911), p. 220. 'Pendant la suspension des hostilités, Tobback voit, – spectacle que la plume se refuse presque á rappeler –, des indigènes, que le festin de la nuit a mis en appetit, ronger des tibias decharnés, et sucer des fonds de cervelles....'

3 A letter from Thys to Philippe Bunau-Varilla dated 8 December 1903 shows the friendship between the two (in the use of 'tu' instead of 'vous'). BV Papers, Box 7. Cornet, *Bataille*, p. 222.

4 Cornet, *Bataille*, p. 194.

5 Ibid., p. 179.

6 Ibid., pp. 183 and 209. The bookkeepers in Loewy's office who died within a short time of arriving in the Congo were: Louis Mossiat, thirty-one years old, of dysentery in April 1897 (after one and one half years of service), Guillaume Dartu, thirty (after seven months of service) in December 1893, and Ernest Schulte, thirty-four, who died of a fever (after only two months on the job in Matadi) in April 1894: *Biographie belge coloniale*, vol. III (Brussels: Librairie Falk et fils, 1948), cols. 641, 258, 793. Also Alfred Scailquin and Jean Groven, who died on 5 June 1898 and 27 May 1895 respectively in Kinkanda on a recreational farm run by the Compagnie du Chemin de Fer and, further, the bookkeepers Louis Dutoit (13 December 1894), Norbert van der Kerckhove (5 December 1894) and Jean Mertens (12 March 1897), III, 789, 390, 383, 481.

7 Cornet, *Bataille*, p. 181.

8 Edmond Picard, *En Congolie*, deuxième édition (Brussels: Paul Lascomblez, 1896), pp. 70–1, 83–4.

9 Cornet, *Bataille*, pp. 179, 184.

10 *Le Mouvement Géographique*, 13e année, no. 52, 6 August 1896, col. 382.

11 Loewy's personal file, Otraco (see note 1).

12 Compagnie du Chemin de Fer du Congo, *Rapport adressé au Conseil d'Administration par l'Administrateur Directeur Général à son retour du Congo, septembre 1896*, seizième fascicule (Brussels: P. Weissenbruch, 1896), pp. 24–5.

13 *Mouvement Géographique*, 15e année, no. 53, 14 August 1896, col. 411.

14 Cornet, *Bataille*, pp. 368–9.

15 Loewy's personal file deposited with Otraco (see note 1). 'Le retour de l'*Albertville*', *La Tribune Congolaise*, jeudi, 10 avril 1902, p. 1, col. 3.

16 Ken Shen Weigh, *Russo-Chinese Diplomacy 1689–1924*, The Russian Series, vol. 3 (Bangor, Maine: University Prints and Reprints, from the edition of 1928), pp. 54–7, 85–94; Chao Yung Seen, *Les Chemins de fer chinois*, Étude historique, politique, économique et financière (Paris: Librairie Technique et Économique, 1938), pp. 145–50; Vera Schmidt, *Die deutsche Eisenbahnpolitik in Shantung 1898–1914: Ein Beitrag zur Geschichte des deutschen Imperialisumus in China*, Veröffentlichungen des Ostasien-Instituts der Ruhr-Universität Bochum (Wiesbaden: Otto Harrassowitz, 1976), pp. 6–33.

17 From a letter of Joseph Loewy's mother-in-law, Mme

Marie Louise Douay, to General Gallieni, Gouverneur militaire de Paris, 10 March 1915, 'Recensement Général des Étrangers', Archives des Yvelines et de l'ancien Département de Seine et Oise.

[18] Régine Kurgan-van Hentenryk, *Léopold II et les groupes financiers belges en Chine. La politique royale et ses prolongements (1895–1914), Mémoires de la classe des lettres*, Collection in-8-2ème serie, T. LXI – Fascicule 2 (Brussels: Palais des Académies, 1972), pp. 98–9.

[19] *North China Herald*, vol. LXXI, no. 1702, 16 October 1903, p. 810, col. 2, shows that Loewy arrived by steamship from Hankow in Shanghai, and vol. LXXI, no. 1709, 27 November 1903, p. 114, col. 3, documents the fact that he left the city to travel to Chefoo. A copy of a letter from Philippe Bunau-Varilla to Georges Espanet, Director of the Imperial Shansi Railway Company in China, dated 8 February 1904, BV Papers, Box 8.

[20] From a letter of M. Verstraete, Ambassade de la République Française, St Petersburg, 19 June 1900, to the French Foreign Minister Delcassé, concerning 'Recrutement du Personnel de la Russo-Chinoise, Mission Spéciale, Direction des Consulates, Sous Direction des offices commercials, No. 156, Chine 402', in the Archives du Ministère des Affaires Étrangères, Paris.

[21] Extract from the Civil Register of the city of Ghent.

[22] Kurgan-van Hentenryk, p. 719. 'An Act to incorporate "Le Crédit Municipal Canadien"', *Statutes of the Province of Québec passed in the Reign of his Majesty King*

Edward the Seventh, Chapter 106 (Quebec: Charles Pageau, 1903), pp. 692–702. *Le Crédit Municipal Canadien, Prospectus* (Quebec: 1904?).

[23] 'Le Résultat d'une volonté sans concessions: La petite histoire de l'électrification dans le Bas St-Laurent', *Revue d'Histoire du Bas St. Laurent*, vol. 3, no. 2 (novembre 1976), pp. 3–10. In September Loewy was officially named Administrateur Directeur Général (see Chapter II, note 7). On 10 October he stopped at the Hotel Viger in Montreal: *Montreal Gazette*, no. 2373, 10 October 1907, p. 3, col. 5. Letters from Joseph Loewy to the town of Rimouski, dated 6 August, 15 October and 1 December 1908 and 4 April 1909, document his presence in Canada (mid-April 1909, even in Rimouski itself): correspondence from the city of Rimouski, Quebec.

[24] Le Crédit Municipal Canadien, Séance du Conseil d'Administration du 29 juin 1909, II, 28, Archives régionales du Québec à Rimouski. Recensement Général des Étrangers, Archives des Yvelines et de l'ancien Département de Seine et Oise. Information from the Archives Cantonales Vaudoises, Lausanne.

4 On the Pirates' Galley

[1] 'Demande de Naturalisation' of Alfred Loewy. (See Chapter 2, note 3).

[2] About the railway Madrid a Cáceres: Francisco Wais San Martin, *Historia General de los Ferrocariles Españolas (1830–1941)* (Madrid: Editorial Nacional, 1967), pp. 230–2.

[3] Letter from Alfred Loewy to

Philippe Bunau-Varilla, 20 March 1902, BV Papers, Box 4. One can only speculate whether Loewy tried to obtain a job with his benefactor for his nephew; Bunau-Varilla carefully pruned his papers before he gave them to the Library of Congress and probably threw out much that he considered insignificant.

[4] *El Sol*, 2 March 1923, p. 4, col. 8.

[5] Cornet, *Bataille*, p. 194.

[6] F.-I. Mouthon, *Du Bluff au Chantage. Les grandes campagnes du 'Matin', Comment on fait l'opinion publique en France*, lre série (Paris: Pauwels, 1908), p. xi.

[7] Letters from Alfred Loewy to Philippe Bunau-Varilla dated 28 April 1901 and 11 February 1907. BV Papers, Box 2 and Box 13.

[8] 'La Visita de Mr Loubet', *La Epoca*, año LVII, Num. 37586, 27 octubre de 1905, p. 2, col. 3.

[9] *New York Herald*, 13 May 1905, p. 20, col. 1.

[10] Alfred Loewy's letter to Philippe Bunau-Varilla, dated The New Willard (Hotel), Washington DC, 13 May 1905. BV Papers, Box 10. Loewy sent Bunau-Varilla the article in the *New York Herald* (see note 9) and it can be assumed that it went to his family in Prague too.

[11] *Briefe an Ottla und die Familie*, ed. H. Binder and K. Wagenbach (Frankfurt un Main: Fischer Verlag, 1981), pp. 88, 93.

5 Kalda Railway, Kafka Railway, Loewy Railway

[1] Mouthon, *Bluff*, p. 28; and Jacques Kayser, *The Dreyfus Affair*, translated from the French by Nora Bickley (New York: Covici,

Friede, Publishers, 1931), p. 44.

[2] Between 1891 and 1894 and especially in the year 1892 the financial situation and the construction problems the Congo Railway encountered were particularly difficult: *Bataille*, p. 218.

[3] Cornet, *Bataille*, pp. 195–7.

6 The Discovery of the New World

[1] The story of Robert's seduction comes from Mrs Klara Kafka de Novy. A number of details of the life of the child point to the fact that the story was known to many of the family members.

[2] School reports and calendars of the Kolin *Gymnasium* and information from the Okresní archiv v Kolíně.

[3] Sources for the information about Otto: 1. Reports of various intelligence agencies (Department of Justice, Military Intelligence, etc.), Classified Subject File, No. 9–16–12–5422, Records of the Department of Justice, Record Group 60, National Archives Washington DC. 2. Otto Kafka's son. 3. 'Register der ertheilten Pässe und Visa von 1890/91 bis 1898' (vol. 737) of the Gesandtschaftsarchiv Paris, Haus-, Hofund Staatsarchiv, Vienna.

[4] Letter of Rufus Sprague, Special Assistant to the Attorney General, Washington DC, dated 5 August 1918, Classified Subject File. (See note 3). Passenger List of the *Pennsylvania*, Records of the Immigration and Naturalization Service, Record Group 85, National Archives Microfilm Publication, T715, Roll 1787.

[5] Circular from the District Court in Jičín, dated 13 September 1906, PŘ, 1921–30, K 615–

20, 1494, Státní ústřední archiv, Prague.

[6] Letter from Otto Kafka to Rufus W. Sprague, Special Assistant to the Attorney-General, NY, dated September 1918, Classified Subject File. (See note 3).

[7] 'Certificado de Acta de Matrimonio' of Otto and Alice Kafka, Department of Health, Commonwealth of Puerto Rico. Memorandum of the War Trade Intelligence and Military Intelligence Bureau (Capt. C.L. Tiffany) to Capt. Roger B. Hull, Naval Intelligence, dated 30 July 1918 and Statement of Otto Kafka to J.W. Kemp and Wm. B. Matthews, special agents, dated 18 August 1918, Classified Subject File. (See note 3).

[8] 'Kafka Threatens Du Pont with Suit', *New York World*, 29 January 1918; 'Names de la Huerta in $2,500,000 Suit', *New York Times*, 13 June 1922, p. 21, col. 8.

[9] Information about Alice Stickney's life and personality from her daughter. 'Kafka Left Family in Want, Wife Says', *New York Times*, 25 November 1923, Section II, p. 1, col. 4; 'Kafka Files Reply to Wife's Charges', *New York Times*, 22 November 1923, p. 14, col. 2.

[10] Passenger List of the *Pennsylvania*, Records (see note 4), T715, Roll 1787. Also 'Report from 1st Class Private Frank Kafka to Major J.B. Ord, dated 26 August 1918, Military Intelligence Division File No. 8576–190, Records of the War Department, General and Special Staffs, Record Group 165, National Archives, Washington DC.

[11] Passenger List of the *Monterey*, Records (see note 4), Microfilm T715, Roll 1882.

[12] Letter from Otto Kafka to Rufus W. Sprague (see note 6).

[13] Passenger List of the *Pretoria*, Records (see note 4), Microfilm T715, Roll 474.

[14] Details of Emil's life in America from his wife, Mrs Elsa Kafka, Chicago.

[15] The photograph of Heinrich Kafka as a soldier comes from Rudolf Kafka's album, which is now in the possession of his children.

7 The Mishpocheh That Stayed at Home

[1] The information about Anna Adler and her husband comes from the following sources: a questionnaire filled out by Ida Bergmann, daughter of Julie Ehrmann (kindly given to me by Klaus Wagenbach); 'Jüdische Kultusgemeinde Strakonitz: Geburtsmatrik Strakonitz vom 1. Nov. 1839 bis 2, November 1861', HBMa 1936, 'Geburts-, Trau- und Sterbe-Matrik, Osek 1803–1839', HBMa 1479, 'Správa matrik židovské náboženské obce v Strakonichích: Matrika zemřelých od r. 1896–1923', HBMa 1943 (all in the Státní ústřední archiv – Archivní správa, Prague); also from the inhabitant registration forms for the city of Prague, 'Popisni arch z roku 1893' (Archiv hlavního města Prahy); PŘ, Pol. Přihlášky, č. krabice: 2, Adámek-Eichler (Státní ústřední archiv, Prague); and *Prager Tagblatt*, no. 209, 8 September 1936, p. 5.

[2] *Prager Tagblatt*, no. 18, 22 January 1921, p. 12, col. 1. Kafka's letter of February 1921 to his sister Ottla is from *Briefe an Ottla* (see ch. IV, note 11).

[3] Particulars about Karoline (Kafka) and Sigmund Kohn from Henry Kafka, London, the son of Rudolf Kafka.

[4] Information about Sigmund Kohn and his brother from his nephew, Walter Kohn.

[5] Quote from Kafka's letter to his parents, 2 to 7 February 1924, generously given to me by Dr Joseph Čermak, the editor of this and other letters from Kafka to his parents.

[6] Particulars about Filip Kafka's businesses from Okresní archiv v Kolíně.

[7] Klaus Wagenbach, *Franz Kafka: Eine Biographie seiner Jugend 1883–1912* (Bern: Francke Verlag, 1958), p. 193.

[8] *Ostrauer Tagblatt*, no. 214, 19 September 1901, p. 3, col. 1.

[9] Friedrich Weihs, *Aus Geschichte und Leben der Teplitzer Judengemeinde (1782–1932)* (Brünn-Prague: Jüdischer Buch- und Kunstverlag, 1932), pp. 42, 59, 75, 91, and Okresní archiv v Teplice.

[10] Details of Josef Poláček's life come to me from his daughter.

[11] Brod, p. 252.

[12] Information about Robert Kafka from Mrs Klara Kafka de Novy.

[13] Brod, pp. 106–7. *Hlád Demokracie*, no. 13, 25 March 1922, p. 2, col. 3.

[14] *Prager Tagblatt*, no. 3, 3 January 1886, Beilage (Supplement), p. 16.

[15] Inhabitant registration forms for the city of Prague, PŘ, Pol. Přihlášky, č. krabice: 245: Kafka, Státní ústřední archiv, Prague.

[16] Passport applications of Hedwig and Lilly Löw, PŘ 1931–40, č. krabice: 8401, L988–92 and 8404, L1001–2, Státní ústřední archiv, Prague.

[17] *Prager Tagblatt*, no. 128, 31 May 1919, p. 7.

[18] *Bericht der Lese- und Redehalle der deutschen Studenten in Prag über das Jahr 1887* (Prague: Selbstverlag, 1888).

[19] Information about Richard Löwy from the City District Committee in Prague I, transmitted to me by the Archivní správa, Prague.

[20] *Prager Tagblatt*, no. 44, 21 February 1922, p. 14.

[21] Information about Max Löwy in the passport documents of the Státní ústřední archiv, Prague, on the printed ballot on display in the Museum of the City of Prague, from the burial records of the Jewish cemetery in Strasnice, and from the Památník Terezín.

8 Lawyers and Factory-Owners

[1] According to the files of the Commercial Court in Prague, Jd. VII, pp. 41, 152, 170, in the Státní archiv, Prague.

[2] *Prager Tagblatt*, no. 240, 31 August 1908, p. 3, col. 2.

[3] *Allg. Adressen-Buch der Königl. Hauptstadt Prag, der Vorstädte Karolinenthal etc.,* (Prague: Verlag der Bohemia, 1875), p. 73; *Adresář Kralovského hlavního mesta Prahy,* ed. Vaclav Leser (Prague: Nakladem Duchoduv obce Prazske, 1891), p. 290.

[4] *Allg. Adressen-Buch*, 1 Theil (1878), p. 51; *Adresář* (1884), p. 188.

[5] Wagenbach, *Biographie*, pp. 240–1.

[6] *Prager Tagblatt*, no. 40, 2 February 1908, p. 8; no. 319, 20 November 1917, p. 8.

[7] *Deutsche Zeitung Bohemia*, no. 115, 16 May 1924, p. 4, col. 3.

[8] Commercial Court files of Hermann Kafka's firm, A XIII 45, Státní archiv (now in the Státní ústřední archiv), Prague. A letter from Moritz, dated 4 July 1883, states that Hermann Kafka had to be absent from Prague on 3 July and consequently could not accede to the wishes of the court to appear before it. If this is true, then possibly Hermann Kafka was not in Prague at the birth of his son.

[9] Robert Mayr, 'Bruno Kafka: Ein Nachruf', *Prager juristische Zeitschrift*, vol. 11, no. 17, 1 October 1931, col. 593 & fol.; *Prager Presse*, no. 188, 14 July 1931, p. 3. Bruno's father-in-law, Maximilian Bondy-Bondrop, was an engineer and director of the firm Moritz Bondy: *Prager Tagblatt*, no. 234, 10 October 1931, pp. 14–15.

[10] 'Nachruf', col. 593.

[11] *Berichte der Lese- und Redehalle.* (See Chapter 7, note 18.)

[12] From information supplied to me by Henry Kafka, London.

[13] Particulars about Kafka's involvement in the firm go back to Commercial Court files of the Prager Asbestwerke Hermann & Co. (Abt. VI, Rg A V–254), which I discovered in the Státní archiv, Prague in 1973.

[14] Information about Leopold Hermann's financial commitment comes to me from Mrs Sue Sinek. His address on the inhabitant registration card (PŘ, Pol. Přihlášky, 1910–53, Hermann, Leopold, Státní ústřední archiv, Prague) is given as Žižkov, Number 918, the same number given for the factory. Franz Kafka, *Schriften, Tagebücher, Briefe Kritische Ausgabe,* ed. Jürgen Born, Gerhard Neumann, Malcolm Pasley and Jost Schillemeit in consultation with Nahum Glatzer, Rainer Gruenter, Paul Raabe and Marthe Robert: *Tagebücher,* ed. Hans-Gerd Koch, Michael Müller and Malcom Pasley, vol. I (Frankfurt am main: S. Fischer Verlag, 1990), pp. 699–702.

[15] Information about Karl Hermann from Vera Saudkova.

[16] From the Commercial Court file. (See note 13.)

[17] Rechenschaftsbericht [Report on Activity] of the Chairman C. Mysyk on the meeting of the 'Vereins der deutschen Beamten der Arbeiter-Unfall-Versicherungsanstalt für das Königreich Böhmen in Prag' held on 9 January 1912, written for the Imperial Royal Police Directorate, Prague, and dated 17 January 1912, PP 1908–15 V10/110, Státní ústřední archiv, Prague. Kafka and Alois Gütling are listed as treasurers of the organization.

[18] Brod, p. 116.

[19] Translated from a letter written by Franz Kafka dated 24 November 1919, in Klaus Wagenbach, 'Julie Wohryzek, die zweite Verlobte Kafkas', *Kafka Symposion,* Sonderreihe dtv 77 (München: Deutscher Taschenbuch Verlag GmbH & Co. KG, 1969), pp. 37 & 39. A photo of Julie Wohryzek, which was generously given to me by her nephew, appears here for the first time.

Acknowledgement

Much of the research for this book was made possible by grants from the Harvey T. Reid Summer Study Fund (Acadia University) and the Social Sciences and Humanities Research Council of Canada.

Photographic Acknowledgements

Sears, Roebuck & Co, Chicago: 62–63 (all); *Compass*, Vienna, 1912, 111; Mrs Elsa Kafka, 60; the children of Otto Kafka, 52, 73, 77; the children of Rudolf Kafka, 61, 64, 65, 72; *Le Congo illustré*, Brussels, 1893, 17; City Planning Office, Prague-Žižkov: 94 (both), 95 (bottom); Státni ústředni archiv, Prague, 85, 89, 92; Státni archiv, Prague (now in the Státni ústředni archiv), 93; Mrs Sue Sinek, 86; Musée de l'Afrique Centrale, Tervuren, Belgium: 14, 16, 20–21 (all), 24, 25, 26 (middle and bottom), 40, 43, 44; Library of Congress, Washington D.C.: 10, 33, 35, 39, 64, 65, 72; the nephew of Julie Wohryzek, 100 (right). The above photos were researched by Anthony Northey.

The author would like to thank the following for their generosity in supplying photographs:
Hartmut Binder Archive, Schöckingen: 68, 94; Klaus Wagenbach, frontispiece, opp. p. 1, 3, 6, 11, 50, 75, 78–79 (all), 81, 83, 84 (all), 100 (left).

Index

Index

Index

Index

KAFKA'S FAMILY TREE BY ANTHON

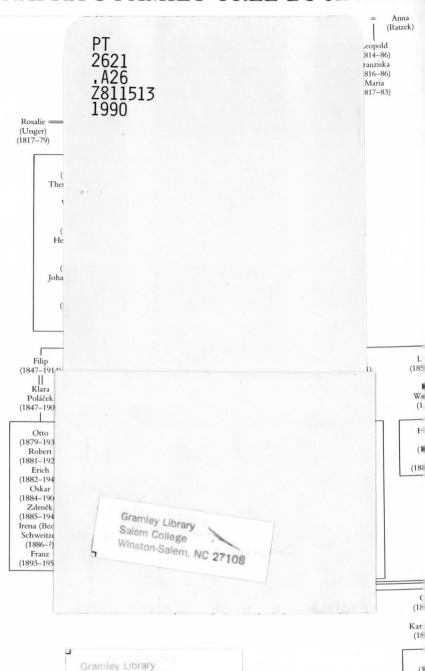

= Anna
(Ratzek)

Leopold
(1814–86)
Franziska
(1816–86)
Maria
(1817–83)

Rosalie =
(Unger)
(1817–79)

Ther

He

Joha

Filip
(1847–191
||
Klara
Poláček
(1847–190

Otto
(1879–193
Robert
(1881–192
Erich
(1882–194
Oskar
(1884–190
Zdeněk
(1885–194
Irena (Be
Schweitz
(1886–?)
Franz
(1893–195

L
(185

W
(1

H

(

(18

C
(18

Kar
(18